Pre-intermediate

Quick Work

A short course in Business English

Vicki Hollett

OXFORD

SECTION	INPUT TEXT	LANGUAGE WORK	OUTPUT TASK
Opinions	**Reading** • political leaflet and encyclopedia entry	Opinions and agreement	Giving and asking for opinions
Agreeing and disagreeing	**Listening** • three discussions about pricing policy	Softening language, expressing tentativeness, and rephrasing	Expressing agreement and disagreement
Holding a meeting	**Reading** • information on traffic problems around the world	Revision	Holding a meeting to generate ideas

4 EXCHANGING INFORMATION   page 36

Explanations	**Listening and reading** • product information and crossword	Getting your meaning across when you don't know a word Pronouncing the alphabet	Describing and explaining products
Checking information	**Listening** • extracts from telephone calls, checking what was said	Checking, repeating, and confirming	Checking you've understood what was said
Updating	**Listening** • series of voicemail messages	Present perfect tense	Providing an information update
Getting the facts	**Listening** • telephone call about missing materials	Phrases for telephoning Polite intonation	Collecting information about a business problem
Doing research	**Reading** • company sales catalogue and purchase request form	Revision	Conducting research into products availability

5 SOLVING PROBLEMS   page 44

Anticipating problems	**Reading** • article about Nintendo	Making predictions *will / won't*	Anticipating problems and planning how to deal with them
Identifying causes	**Listening** • discussion of why an advertisement wasn't effective	Making deductions *must be / can't be / could be / might be*	Identifying the causes of international business problems
Considering alternatives	**Listening** • discussion of integrated business software	*if-* sentences	Considering alternative courses of action and their consequences
Implementing	**Listening** • allocating tasks at a meeting	Allocating tasks, talking about schedules	Deciding how to implement your plans
Planning strategy	**Reading and listening** • items in an in-tray and voicemail message	Revision	Planning a company's future strategy

INFORMATION FILES   page 54   **GLOSSARY**   page 68

TAPESCRIPT   page 62

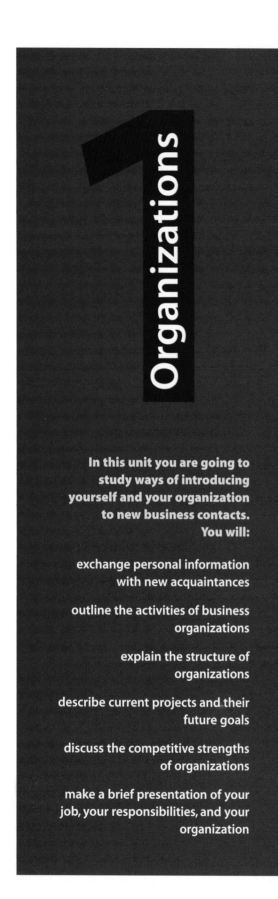

1 Organizations

In this unit you are going to study ways of introducing yourself and your organization to new business contacts. **You will:**

exchange personal information with new acquaintances

outline the activities of business organizations

explain the structure of organizations

describe current projects and their future goals

discuss the competitive strengths of organizations

make a brief presentation of your job, your responsibilities, and your organization

▶ MEETING PEOPLE

1 Introduce yourself to another student.

Hello, / Hi, nice to meet you. *I'm ...*
I come from / I'm from ... *I work for ...*

2 ⌷1.1⌷ These people all need English for their work. Listen and find out why. Answer the questions.

Alessandro Ponti

a How often does Alessandro take English lessons?
b What does he do in his free time?

Michiko Sudo

c How many employees does Michiko's company have?
d What's she responsible for?

Peter Leutwiler

e What does Peter do?
f Where does he live?

Jean-Philippe Gérard

g Who does Jean-Philippe work for?
h What subject does he study?

Sushma Advani

i Where does Sushma come from?
j Who is her company's main client?

KEY VOCABULARY

a colleague a person who works with you in the same organization or group

an employee a person who works for an organization

freelance working for several different employers and being paid separately for each piece of work

responsible for having the job of looking after something, in charge of

a plant a large factory

a recruitment agency a company that finds new employees for other companies

3 1.1 Listen again. Which person needs English to:

a   travel abroad?
b   recruit foreign employees?
c   communicate with colleagues?
d   talk to customers?
e   read books?

What about you? Why do you need English for your work?

Present simple

We add *s* to the third person singular form of the Present simple tense.

I / You / We / They   employ 320 people.
He / She / It   employ**s** 320 people.

We use *do* and *does* to make questions.

*Where **do** you / **does** she live?*
*Who **do** they / **does** he work for?*
*What **do** you / **does** it do?*

We use *don't* and *doesn't* to make negatives.

*I / You / We / They **don't** live in Mumbai any more.*
*He / She **doesn't** live in Mumbai any more.*

---

4 1.1 Listen again and complete these sentences.

a   Alessandro Ponti is .... research technician at a hospital in Torino. He .... English lessons twice a week so he can communicate better with his colleagues.

b   Michiko Sudo .... in her family's trading company. She .... responsible .... worldwide sales and marketing.

c   Peter Leutwiler is a .... computer consultant. He .... in database management for banking and financial services.

d   Jean-Philippe Gérard works .... Eco Industries SA. He also .... engineering at the Université de Technologie.

e   Sushma Advani .... five languages at work. She works for a .... agency in Pittsburgh.

Output task

1 Find out about some other students. Ask and answer these questions.

–   Where do you live?
–   Where do you come from?
–   Who do you work for?
–   What does your company do?
–   How many employees does it have?
–   Who are your main customers?
–   What are you responsible for?
–   Are you married?
–   Do you have any children?
–   What do you like doing in your free time?

2 When you have finished, report back to the class.

▶ COMPANIES

1 Do you know any of these companies? What products and services do they sell?
Are any of them in the same business as you? Where are their headquarters located?

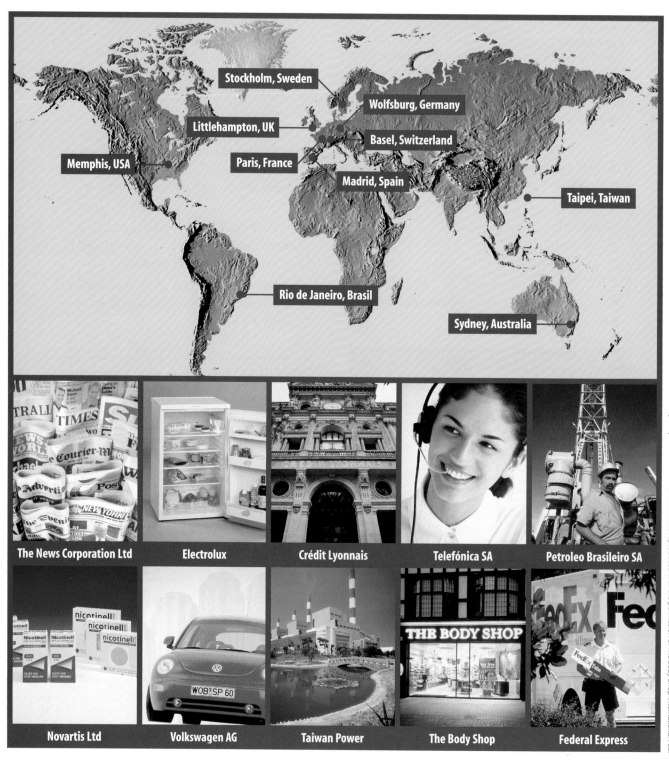

2 What type of businesses are they? Find:

a   a car manufacturer
b   a publisher
c   a freight company
d   a bank
e   a pharmaceutical company
f   a telecommunications company
g   a petroleum company
h   an electricity company
i   a retailer
j   a white goods producer.

3 What does each company do? Find one which:

a   develops drugs and medicines
b   publishes newspapers and operates TV networks
c   sells skin and hair care products
d   delivers mail, packages, and freight
e   explores for oil and operates refineries
f   manufactures cars
g   produces refrigerators, freezers, etc.
h   provides commercial banking services
i   supplies electricity
j   supplies telephone and cable services.

4 Complete these sentences about some other companies using words from the list. The first one has been done for you.

publishes	*produces*	manufactures	sells
provides	delivers	develops	transports

a   BASF *produces* chemicals, but it's best known for its audio and video tapes.

b   Hitachi Ltd, Tokyo, was founded in 1910 and it .... electrical machinery and semiconductors.

c   Carrefour SA is a French retail organization. It .... a wide range of products in hypermarkets in nine different countries.

d   Lloyd's of London opened more than 300 years ago and it .... insurance services for clients in more than 100 countries.

e   The United States Postal Service processes, transports, and .... 182 billion pieces of mail a year – 40% of the world's total.

f   Reed Elsevier's head office is based in the UK and it .... journals, magazines, books, and regional newspapers.

g   R&D is important at 3M and the company .... many new products. In fact, 30% of the company's revenue comes from products introduced in the last four years.

Output task

1 Tell a partner about your company.

–   What business is it in?
–   What does it do?
–   Who are its main clients?
–   When was it founded?
–   Where's the head office based?
–   Where does it operate?

2 See how much you can remember. Take it in turns to talk about each other's companies. Help your partner and correct any mistakes.

You work for an engineering company?
    Yes, that's right.

Your company builds locomotives?
    No, that's not quite right. We build locomotive engines.

QUICK CHECK

Can you talk about countries and nationalities in English? Answer these questions and check.

1   What country do you come from? What's your nationality?

2   Name your neighbouring countries. What nationalities are the people who live there?

3   What other countries do you have business dealings with? What nationalities are your business contacts?

▶ COMPANY ACTIVITIES

1 Study the structure of this organization. Find out the meaning of any unknown words. Say what the different departments do.

OPERATIONS

a   Production
b   Research and Development
c   Quality
d   Logistics
e   Production Planning

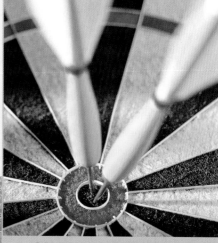

SALES AND MARKETING

a   Sales
b   Market Research
c   Marketing
d   After-sales
e   Advertising

FINANCE

a   Purchasing
b   Finance
c   Bookkeeping

HUMAN RESOURCES

a   Salaries
b   Recruitment
c   Personnel
d   Training

SUPPORT SERVICES

a   Legal Affairs
b   Security
c   Maintenance
d   Public Relations

2 Look at Operations. Find the department which:

1 invents new products and improves existing products
2 prepares schedules for manufacturing the products
3 manufactures the products
4 organizes transport and distributes the products
5 designs and implements procedures to ensure the products meet specifications and there are no mistakes.

3 Look at Human Resources. Find the department which:

1 hires new employees
2 runs courses for the employees
3 pays the employees
4 keeps employees' records and deals with any problems employees have.

4 Look at Finance. Find the department which:

1 keeps records of all the money coming into and going out of the company
2 buys raw materials from suppliers
3 keeps accounts, plans cash flow, and manages investments.

5 Look at Sales and Marketing. Find the department which:

1 positions products in the market to attract customers
2 collects information about potential customers and what they want
3 writes and places ads for products in magazines, newspapers, etc.
4 sells the products
5 deals with problems and complaints from customers.

6 Look at Support Services. Find the department which:

1 protects the company from loss and theft
2 services the machines and equipment and looks after the buildings
3 provides advice and answers questions about the law and contracts
4 deals with the press.

Word stress

When you're learning new words, it often helps to make a note of their pronunciation. What different methods are used to record the stress in these words? Which method do you prefer?

pro'duction, 'maintenance, perso'nnel

production (oOo), maintenance (Ooo), personnel (ooO)

pro<u>duc</u>tion, <u>main</u>tenance, person<u>nel</u>

Check your dictionary and see how it records the stress of words. What other information does it give about pronunciation?

Output task

1 Draw a diagram of your organization. Prepare to answer questions about it, e.g.

– What departments, divisions, and sections does your company have?
– How is the work organized?
– What does each section do?
– How are the sections linked to each other?

2 Work with a partner. Take it in turns to show each other your diagrams and explain how your companies work. Talk about the activities of each section.

▶ CURRENT PROJECTS

1 `1.2` Listen to five people talking about their company's current projects. Match each one to the right picture.

1 ....
2 ....
3 ....
4 ....
5 ....

A

D

B

E

C

KEY VOCABULARY

a component one of the parts of a product

a cure medicine or treatment that makes a sick person healthy again

data information

a gene part of a cell of a living thing which controls its development

inventory stocks, a supply of things you need

to install to put equipment in place so it's ready for use

labour costs money that must be paid to workers

to lay to put something in the correct position for a particular purpose

to recycle to use again

to be scrapped to be thrown away because it's no longer useful

to set up to start, to establish

a warehouse a large building where goods are stored

Present tenses, *going to*

We use the Present simple tense to talk about things we do all the time.

*We **provide** telephone services.*
*We **do** genetic research.*

We use the Present continuous tense to talk about temporary activities and projects that are in progress now.

*We**'re laying** cables across the country.*
*We**'re trying** to identify the genes that cause high blood pressure.*

We use *going to* to talk about future plans and intentions.

*We**'re going to** offer our customers TV services.*
*One day we**'re going to** find a cure.*

2 Match these pairs of sentences with the correct explanation.

a   I'm working for Cisco.
b   I work for Cisco.

c   He's speaking Italian.
d   He speaks Italian.

e   We're staying at the Sheraton.
f   We stay at the Sheraton.

1   It's a temporary job.
2   It's a permanent job.

3   It's something he can do when he needs to.
4   He's on the phone to a client in Italy.

5   It's the hotel we always use when we go to New York.
6   It's the hotel we're in at the moment.

3 1.2 Listen again. Make a note of one thing each company *is doing* now and one thing it's *going to do* in the future.

Output task

1 Prepare to describe your company or your department's current projects. Make some brief notes about:

– what you're doing now
– what you're going to do in the future.

2 Work with a partner. Take it in turns to describe the projects. Answer any questions your partner may have.

QUICK CHECK

Can you talk about numbers and times in English? Follow these instructions and check.

1   Say these numbers: 7, 12, 14, 40, 100, 105.
2   Say your telephone and fax numbers.
3   Say today's date.
4   Say the year you were born.
5   Say what time it is.

6   Say these prices:

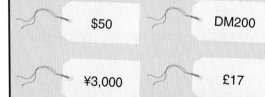

$50   DM200   ¥3,000   £17

7   The first month of the year is January. Name the other eleven.
8   The first day of the week is Monday. Name the other six.
9   The first season of the year is spring. Name the other three.

▶ COMPANY STRENGTHS

1 What airlines do you like to fly with, and why? What makes a good airline?

2 Quickly read through this article about Southwest, an American airline. Find three things that make Southwest special.

3 Read the article again with a partner. Find as many different ways as you can to complete these sentences.

a One of the things that makes Southwest profitable is ...
b One of the main things that attracts passengers to Southwest is ...
c One of the best things about working for Southwest is ...
d One of the most unusual things about Southwest is ...

4 Practise pronouncing the numbers in the article with a partner. Take it in turns to ask and answer these questions.

a What are Southwest's revenues?
b How many airports does it serve?
c How many planes does it have?
d How many flights does it make a day?
e What type of aeroplane does Southwest fly?
f How long does it take to get a Southwest plane ready to fly?
g How many employees does Southwest have?

5 Discuss these questions with a partner. Do you agree with each other?

a Would you like to invest in Southwest Airlines? Why / Why not?
b Would you like to fly on a Southwest flight? Why / Why not?
c Would you like to work for Southwest? Why / Why not?

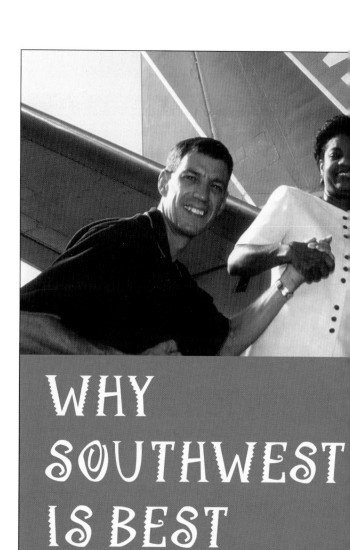

WHY SOUTHWEST IS BEST

The business

Southwest Airlines is the fourth largest airline in the US, with revenues of $4.1 billion. It serves fifty-four airports with nearly 300 planes and makes 2,400 flights per day. The company regularly wins awards for having the most satisfied customers and the best record for landing on time. Southwest is the only American airline to make a profit every year for the last twenty-six years. Southwest only flies one type of aeroplane (a 737), so Southwest mechanics are very quick. They get the planes ready to fly in just twenty minutes – the industry average is more than one hour. The company employs 27,000 people and the company's Chairman, Herb Kelleher, knows many of their names and something about them too. He frequently asks employees about their children, husbands or wives, or hobbies.

Southwest Airlines flight attendants often make up songs that they sing to passengers. Here's one, sung to the tune of *Crazy* by Patsy Cline:

'You're crazy, for flying other airlines. Crazy for paying those rip-off fares. We're the only airline that loves you. Save money and fly Southwest Air.'

The service

Southwest's passengers usually call the airline directly to book their flights, or they book by email – the company doesn't use many agents' reservations systems. A lot of passengers travel with no tickets and no seat assignments – it's first-come, first-served. Southwest usually flies short-haul flights that only take about an hour. The airline doesn't offer a meal service, but its prices are competitive and passengers love the low fares. Southwest Airlines employees like to have fun. For example, flight attendants make their own fancy dresses for holidays – dressing up like turkeys at Thanksgiving, and wearing Santa Claus hats at Christmas.

The employees

When things get busy, Southwest employees do work that is outside their job description. It's not unusual to see pilots helping ticket agents, or ticket agents loading bags. And Southwest employees can make decisions on their own. They can break company rules at any time if they think it makes good sense. Southwest pays wages that are standard for the industry, but it asks its employees to be more productive. For example, pilots at the biggest airlines fly fifty hours a month but Southwest pilots fly seventy hours. Southwest employees stay with the company a long time; it has the lowest staff turnover in the American airline industry.

When Southwest recruits new employees, it looks for people with a sense of humour.

KEY VOCABULARY

an award a prize for doing something well

a competitive price a cheap and reasonable price

a fare the amount of money you have to pay for a ticket to travel

on time at the correct time, not late

a passenger a person who travels on a plane, in a car, etc.

profit a positive sum of money made by a business, total sales minus total costs

a reservation a booking you make in advance

revenues turnover, total sales

a short-haul flight a flight over a short distance

staff turnover the rate at which employees leave and join a company

Herb Kelleher, the company Chairman, dresses up as Elvis Presley for photo shoots.

Output task

1 Think about why your company is special. Make some brief notes. Is it because:

- you're a market leader in your industry? (Who are your competitors?)
- you have won awards? (What and why?)
- your prices are competitive? (How do you do it?)
- you're better than your competitors somehow? (In what way and why?)
- your employees are unusual in some way? (How?)
- your management is special in some way? (How?)
- there are some other reasons? (What?)

2 Work in small groups. Take it in turns to explain what makes your company special.

▶ COMPANY PRESENTATION

1 Does your company have sister organizations in other countries? How do you communicate with other organizations at home and abroad? What technology do you use?

2 `1.3` Helen Chapelle is Vice-President of JRB, an engineering consultancy company. Listen to her introducing an international meeting and answer these questions.

a Where is the meeting taking place?
b What's it about?

3 `1.3` Listen again. What does Helen say about:

a JRB's globalization programme?
b what the company needs?
c her role in the project?

What other people do you think are attending this meeting?

4 `1.4` Read this list of the other participants at the meeting. Then listen to each person introducing themselves. Match each speaker with the correct name.

a Dr A Binner, Task Co-ordinator, JRB
b R Vermuelen, Quality Management, JRB
c I Töth, Director, Harding Management Consulting, Hungary
d L Peters, Internet Services, Crossnet, UK
e C Mitchell, Keyes Telecom Group, USA

5 `1.4` Listen again and answer these questions.

a What is R Vermuelen working on at the moment and what's he going to do next month?
b What is Crossnet responsible for?
c What's Dr Binner's role in this project?
d What services does Keyes Telecom Group provide?
e What's the main strength of Harding Management Consulting?

Output task

1 Imagine you're going to an international meeting where you need to introduce yourself and your company. Who is going to be at the meeting? What do you need to tell them?

Plan what to say first. You can make brief notes, but don't write sentences. Just write key words or phrases. Here are some possible topics.

2 When you're ready, work in small groups. Take it in turns to give your presentations.

First explain who the audience is that you are speaking to. Then introduce yourself and your organization to the other group members, and answer their questions.

Company name	What makes your company special or unusual
Activities, products, services, etc.	**Your responsibilities**
Facts and figures (employees, revenues, locations, etc.)	**Current projects and future plans**

KEY VOCABULARY

to co-ordinate to organize people so they work together efficiently
to extend to make something bigger or longer
globalization the process of increasing your business operations to cover the world
to guarantee to promise to make sure that something will happen
infrastructure the basic systems an organization needs to function effectively
installation the process of putting equipment in place

so that it's ready for use
a link a connection
ISO 9000 a quality management programme
local knowledge knowledge of a particular region or place
reliable always working well and not likely to fail
a role a function someone has, a part someone plays in a company or project
within budget not spending more money than planned

CHECK OUT

1 In this unit you have studied ways of introducing yourself and your organization to new business contacts. Have you completed all the tasks? Look back at the unit aims on page 4 and tick (✓) the tasks you have done.
2 Which tasks did you find most useful? Why?
3 Which tasks did you find most difficult? Why?
4 Are there tasks you need to study further?

MAKE A NOTE OF
• useful things you want to remember
• difficult things you want to study further

2 Visitors

In this unit you are going to rehearse a visit from foreign business contacts. You will:

tell visitors about your home town

describe a journey

make arrangements for a visit

greet and make conversation with new business acquaintances

describe business or technical processes

show visitors around your place of work

▶ LOCAL INFORMATION

1 Read this fact sheet about Beijing. Can you guess any of the missing information?

Information for travellers:
BEIJING

Population	Approximately _____ people.
Language	The official language is _____. Very few people speak English.
Business hours	Stores usually open at 10.00 and close at _____. A lot of small shops and government offices close at lunch-time between 11.30 and 13.30.
Climate	Springs and autumns are very pleasant. Summers are _____ and winters are cold. _____ a lot in July and August.
Tipping	Tipping is unusual, but in some hotels you need to give a small tip to _____. Just ten yuan★ is enough.
Water	Only drink _____. Don't drink _____.

★*yuan – the basic unit of currency in China*

---

2 What questions could you ask to find out the missing information?
e.g. *What's the population of Beijing?*
You can check your answers in File 2 on page 54.

3 Work with a partner. Ask and answer questions and complete the fact sheet. Here's the missing information – but be careful, it's in the wrong order.

very hot	21.00	water from the tap
11 million	It rains	bottled water
Mandarin	the porters	

4 If you were travelling to Beijing, what other information would you like to know? Think of more questions to ask.

5 2.1 Now listen to a business traveller who is going to Beijing for the first time. Does he ask any of your questions?

6 2.1 Listen again and complete the traveller's questions.

a .... there .... crime in Beijing?

b What kind of clothing .... I take?

c .... business meetings? What do people wear?

d Do .... people .... English?

e Is it difficult .... in Beijing?

f .... at business meetings?

Practise asking and answering the questions with a partner.

7 Complete these sentences about doing business in Beijing. Use *shouldn't* or *don't need to*.

a You .... speak any Mandarin if you have an interpreter. They will translate for you.

b You .... be late for meetings. It's very rude.

c You .... give business cards with just one hand. Two hands is more polite.

d You .... tip taxi drivers because they are not expecting it.

e You .... drink the tap water in case it makes you ill.

f You can tip hotel porters if you like, but you .... tip much. Just ten yuan will do.

Now make up some similar sentences about doing business in your country.

should and *need to*

Should and *need to* have similar meanings in affirmative sentences.

*You **should** take a suit.* (It's the right thing to do.)
*You **need to** be patient.* (It's necessary.)

The negative forms have very different meanings.

*You **shouldn't** try to rush things.* (It's the wrong thing to do.)
*You **don't need to** wear a jacket all the time.* (It's not necessary.)

Output task

1 Someone is coming to visit your town or city on business. What kind of local information would they need? Think of some questions they could ask. You can use the ideas below or think of other topics.

the population	the currency
the language	business hours
the weather	business meetings
the food	the water
tipping	crime

2 When you have planned some questions, work with a partner. One person is the visitor and the other is the host or hostess. Practise asking and answering the questions.

QUICK CHECK

Check you know the question words in English. List question words that begin with *Wh*.

When   Wh ...

Now list expressions that begin with *How*.

How many   How ...

▶ **JOURNEYS**

1 Do you travel a lot on business? And what about for pleasure? Ask and answer these questions with a partner.

a   What's the longest trip you've ever made?
b   How did you travel?
c   How long did the journey there take?

What's the difference between *trip, travel*, and *journey*? If you're not sure, check the definitions in File 16 on page 61.

2 Read this article about Nick Sanders and find out why he looks a little tired.

Simple past

In the Simple past tense, regular verbs end in -*ed*.

monitor – monitored   *travel – travelled*
supply – supplied   *include – included*

If a verb ends with a /d/ or /t/ sound, the past form is pronounced with a long /ɪd/ ending.

included   ɪnˈkluːdɪd
completed   kəmˈpliːtɪd

A lot of common English verbs, and some modal verbs, have irregular past tense forms.

have – had   *take – took*   *send – sent*
can – could   *must – had to*

We use *did* to make past tense questions and negatives.

*How many countries **did** Nick visit?*
*Nick **didn't** break any speed limits.*

E v e n t   h o r i z o n ············

Triumphant biker returns

If Nick Sanders looks tired, it's because he's just been on a very long journey – all around the world. Nick successfully completed the Mobil Challenge and became the fastest person ever to circle the globe overland on a motor vehicle. He travelled 29,000 km across four continents in less than thirty-two days.

The route included the UK, France, Italy, Switzerland, Germany, the Czech Republic, Slovakia, Hungary, Romania, Bulgaria, Turkey, India, Thailand, Malaysia, Singapore, Australia, New Zealand, Canada, the USA, Portugal, and Spain – twenty-one countries in all.

Nick drove a regular production model Triumph Daytona motorcycle, but he took a lot of high-tech equipment along with him. IBM supplied him with a Thinkpad computer and a wireless telephone link so that he could connect to the Internet. And he had a Panasonic digital camera so that he could send pictures of his trip to a website at night. Guinness monitored his progress with a Global Positioning System unit on the bike. It relayed his position to a satellite every hour.

3 Ask and answer these questions with a partner.

a What record does Nick Sanders hold?
b How long did it take him to travel round the world?
c How many countries did he travel through?
d How did he get from Singapore to Australia?
e What equipment did he take and why?

4 Complete Nick's story using verbs from the boxes below. Remember to put the verbs into the past tense.

get   rise   take   slow   can't   be   must

India .... the most difficult country for Nick. It was very hot and temperatures .... to 42°C. The local traffic was bad and it .... him down. He .... keep going to break the record, so he .... stop very often. He only .... short naps so he .... very tired.

be   hit   wake up   risk   fall   catch   manage   race

Once he .... asleep momentarily when he was driving. Luckily he .... almost immediately and .... to stop. He never .... going over the speed limit in case the police .... him, but in some parts of Australia, there .... no speed limits, so he .... the accelerator and .... along at 200 km per hour.

Output task

1 You are going to describe a trip you have made. It could be a business trip or another type of journey. Think about:

- where you went and why
- how you travelled and how long it took
- what you took with you
- how you communicated with home
- the problems you had en route.

2 Work with a partner or in small groups. Take it in turns to tell each other about your trips.

▶ MAKING ARRANGEMENTS

1 When you go on business trips, who makes the arrangements for you? Do you ever plan trips for other people?

2 [2.2] Louise Roxton is going on a business trip to France. Look at her itinerary below, then listen to a telephone conversation about it. Make any necessary additions or changes to the itinerary.

ITINERARY

Tuesday

Morning
09.00   Arrival in St Egrève
            Coffee with Nathalie Rousseau (Chief Operating Officer)
            Meetings with the marketing team

Afternoon
            Grenoble facility tour

Evening
20.00   Dinner at a seafood restaurant with Antoine Boirin

Wednesday

Morning
09.30   Visit to clients – Morin Pharmaceutique

Afternoon

Evening

Present continuous

We use the Present continuous tense to talk about planned future arrangements.

You're **visiting** one of our clients on Wednesday morning.
You're **not doing** anything in the afternoon.

3 Look at the revised itinerary and say what Louise is doing.

She's arriving at ten o'clock on Tuesday.
She's having coffee with ...

4 Compare these invitations. Which one is more formal?

Do you want to see round the Grenoble facility?
Would you like to go to a Thai restaurant?

Work with a partner. Respond to questions a–f with invitations or offers. Each time, begin *Yes, would you like to ...?* or *Yes, do you want to ...?*

Have you got a moment?
    Yes, would you like to talk to me?
    Yes, do you want to talk to me?

a   Is this your mobile phone?
b   Is anyone else getting hungry?
c   Are you going for a drink after work?
d   Do you have a pen in your bag?
e   Is this seat free?
f   Have you finished with this newspaper?

5 Now think of more replies, but this time offer help with: *Yes, would you like me to ...?* or *Yes, do you want me to ...?*

Is that door open?
    Yes, would you like me to close it?
    Yes, do you want me to close it?

a   Are you going to the Post Office?
b   Are you driving to the conference?
c   Is anyone else in here a little cold?
d   Did you go to the meeting last Friday?
e   Is this your bag on the floor?
f   Is that Bill Gates over there?

6 Now think of polite replies to these statements. Each time, begin *Would you like (me) to ...?* or *Do you want (me) to ...?*

a   This bag is pretty heavy.
b   Someone said you're playing golf this weekend.
c   That cake looks nice.
d   My car won't start.
e   I must call my office.
f   Oh, no! I've forgotten my credit card!

7 ☐2.2☐ Listen again to Louise's replies. What does she say when Jean-François:

a says she's arriving at nine o'clock?
b invites her to see round the Grenoble facility?
c mentions a seafood restaurant?
d suggests a Thai restaurant instead?
e mentions she's visiting Morin Pharmaceutique?
f offers to cancel Morin Pharmaceutique?
g suggests a city tour?
h says he'll arrange it?

8 Work with a partner. Act out a similar conversation to the one on the recording. Look at the itinerary opposite to help you.

Invitations and offers

We generally show enthusiasm when we accept invitations and offers.

Do you want me to arrange a tour?
Yes, please. I'd like that.
That sounds nice.
That'd be very nice.

We often apologize and provide an explanation when we refuse.

I'm afraid I won't have time.
I'm sorry, but I have to leave by six.

And of course we thank people for their help.

Would you like me to call you a taxi?
Thanks a lot.
That's very kind of you.

Output task

1 Practise making arrangements with a partner. One person is A and the other is B. Follow the instructions in the boxes.

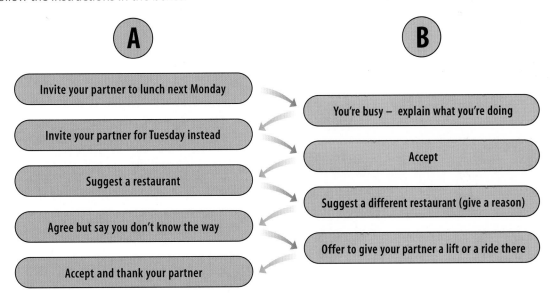

A

- Invite your partner to lunch next Monday
- Invite your partner for Tuesday instead
- Suggest a restaurant
- Agree but say you don't know the way
- Accept and thank your partner

B

- You're busy – explain what you're doing
- Accept
- Suggest a different restaurant (give a reason)
- Offer to give your partner a lift or a ride there

2 Now have a similar conversation with your partner. This time, make arrangements to visit a local tourist attraction.

▶ FIRST MEETINGS

1 Look at the cartoon. Think of suitable replies to the questions the people in the picture are asking.

2 Now match these replies with the questions.

a You, too.
b No, they're free.
c Not too bad, thanks.
d Yes, I'm looking forward to it.
e Please do.
f It's OK, thanks, I can manage.
g Yes, it was dreadful!
h No, sorry, I'm not.
i No, it's going to be twenty minutes late.
j I'm afraid not.
k No, just a few minutes.
l I'd prefer a gin and tonic.

3 Could you ask foreign visitors to your country these questions? Try to think of more questions you could ask. Add them to the table.

Topic	Yes / No **questions**	Wh- **questions**
The weather	It's a nice day today, isn't it?	What was the weather like in … when you left?
Their journey	Did you have a good trip? Did you have any trouble finding your way?	How long did it take? What time did you leave?
Their family	Are you married? Do you have any children / brothers / sisters? Have they started school / university yet? Do you have any pets?	What does your husband / wife do? How old are they? What subjects are they studying?
Their job and career	Have you worked for … for long? Do you travel a lot on business?	How long have you been working for …? Where did you work before?
Their hobbies and interests	Are you interested in music / sport …? Do you take part in any sports?	What kind of music / movies / books do you like? Where do you play / go …?

Question forms

We often start conversations with *Yes / No* questions.

Is this your first visit to London?
Do you live in the centre of the city?

Then we continue with *Wh-* or *How* questions.

When were you here last?
How long does it take you to get to work?

Output task

1 Work with a partner. Act out a situation where two business contacts meet for the first time at an airport, and then go out for dinner. One person is the host, the other is the visitor.

Host
Welcome your visitor to your country.
Ask about their journey.
Offer to help with their bags.
Find out if there is anything your visitor needs to do immediately – use the telephone, change money, etc.
Make conversation with your visitor in the taxi to the restaurant. Ask about their:
– job and career
– family
– hobbies and interests.

Visitor
Respond politely to your host's questions. Try to keep the conversation going smoothly.

2 When you have finished, change roles and act out the conversation again.

▶ SHOWING VISITORS ROUND

1 What type of car do you drive? What is important to you when you are choosing a car? Is it speed, size, price, or other qualities?

2 2.3 Listen to a project manager describing the process of developing a new car. Number the photos in the right order.

a
Testing the fibreglass model in a wind tunnel

b
Going into production

c
Testing the car over different road conditions

d
Testing the clay model in a wind tunnel

e
Building a clay model

f
Creating 3D computer models

g
Building a full-size fibreglass model

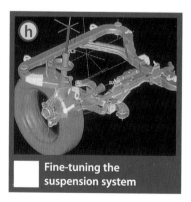

h
Fine-tuning the suspension system

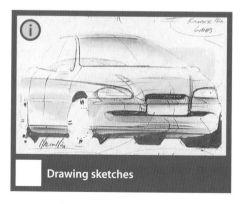

i
Drawing sketches

KEY VOCABULARY

aerodynamics the study of the way things move through the air

an assembly line a sequence of machines and workers making a product on a moving belt

a buck a piece (informal) a dollar for each one

a bumper a metal or plastic bar at the front and back of a car that protects it in small accidents

CAD-CAM computer-aided design, computer-aided manufacturing

an envelope a paper pocket for sending letters

fibreglass a hard material

made from plastic and glass fibres

to fine-tune to make very small changes to something until it works perfectly

market research the study of what people want to buy and why

prospective buyers people who might buy products in the future

a sketch a quick drawing without much detail

sophisticated advanced and complicated

a stage a group of actions or steps in a process

a step one action in a process

Passives

Notice the two forms of the verb *build* in these sentences.

*Robots **build** the cars.* (active verb form)
*The cars are **built** by robots.* (passive verb form)

To say what people or things do, we use the active verb form. To say what happens to people or things, we use the passive verb form.

We often use passive verb forms when we're interested in an action but not interested in who performs it.

*The car **is tested** on a track in Death Valley.*

To form the passive, we use the appropriate form of the verb *be* and the past participle form of the main verb.

*This model **was shown** to prospective buyers last week.*

3 [2.3] Listen again and answer these questions.

a What kinds of early calculations are made by the computers?
b Why is clay used to make the first model?
c Who is the fibreglass model shown to?
d What else is the fibreglass model used for?
e Where are the real cars tested and why?
f How are the cars built?

4 [2.3] Listen to the phrases the manager uses to explain the sequence of the actions in the process. Complete these sentences.

a ……… ……… ……… ……… a basic idea – a few sketches on the back of an envelope.
b ……… ……… ……… is to make a clay model of the car.
c ………, ……… ………, we build a fibreglass model.
d It's too late to make major changes to the design ……… ……… ……… .
e Yes, production's ……… ……… ……… .

Output task

1 Think of a process in your workplace and prepare to describe it. This could be the development of a new product, how you order goods, how you make payments, how you manufacture products, or any other process.

Make a list of the different steps or stages in the process. Think about how you will:
– describe what happens at each step or stage
– explain the sequence of the actions.

2 When you're ready, work with a partner or in small groups. Take it in turns to describe your processes and answer questions.

▶ COMPANY VISIT

1 Have you ever heard of Intuit, the producers of Quicken® and other business and accounting software? Read one of their webpages describing a special company event. Who attends the event and why?

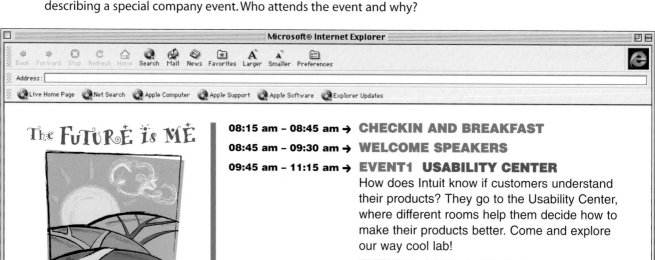

The FUTURE is ME

and the CHOICES are MINE

Every year, the third Thursday in April is national 'Take your daughter to work day' in the US. Over the last five years, millions of girls have gone to work with an adult to learn more about what their parents do and the different career paths available to them. Take Our Daughters To Work Day® was created so we could help girls stay confident and strong.

Many companies now organize special events like this one. All daughters, cousins, nieces, and granddaughters are invited to Intuit, the producer of Quicken®, and other personal and small business finance software and Internet services, to receive breakfast, lunch and the chance to explore the company campus.

08:15 am – 08:45 am → CHECKIN AND BREAKFAST

08:45 am – 09:30 am → WELCOME SPEAKERS

09:45 am – 11:15 am → EVENT1 USABILITY CENTER

How does Intuit know if customers understand their products? They go to the Usability Center, where different rooms help them decide how to make their products better. Come and explore our way cool lab!

EVENT2 COPY CENTER

Check out our giant photocopier and supply of color paper. Take home a special gift for Mom on Mother's Day.

EVENT3 PB&J EXTRAVAGANZA

How do you tell a computer what to do? How do you make a peanut butter and jelly sandwich? Come and find out from Kathy and Kristin, who will tell us how to talk to a computer and make a good old-fashioned PB&J.

EVENT4 SOUND LAB

Explore the world of sound with Mark and see how we use sound effects in our products.

EVENT5 QUICKEN® DEMO

If you're a teenager between the ages of 13 and 19, Rod will explain the basics of Quicken®. Find out how to manage your allowance and babysitting money.

EVENT6 CAREER FAIR

How can I prepare for college? WHAT is a resumé and WHY do I need one? Some of Intuit's best employees will answer these questions and more at the career fair.

11:30 am – 12:30 pm → LUNCH

Join us in the cafeteria to find out the menu surprises we have planned for all of the daughters, nieces, cousins, and granddaughters here at Intuit today.

2 Discuss these questions with some other students.

a What do you think is the purpose of Take Our Daughters To Work Day®? Do you think it's a good idea?

b Do you think it's fair to invite the daughters but not the sons?

c What different things can girls do at Intuit?

d Would you like to have a Take Your Child To Work Day in your company? Why/Why not?

e If you wanted to organize a similar event at your company, what would you show the children? What parts of your workplace and activities would you want your young guests to see?

KEY VOCABULARY

an allowance a small amount of money given to a child by its parents, usually on a regular basis (in UK English, *pocket money*)
a demo an abbreviation for *a demonstration*
an extravaganza a very entertaining event

a lab an abbreviation for *a laboratory*
a resumé a written account of your education and work experience, often used when applying for a job
way cool very fashionable and popular

Output task

1 Do you ever receive foreign visitors at your place of work? Who are they and why do they come? Do you ever visit business contacts abroad? Who do you visit and why?

2 Work with a partner. Imagine you are expecting a visit from a foreign business contact and create the scenario. Decide:

– who the visitor could be (what company they work for and their job)
– the purpose of their visit
– the people they want to meet
– the information they want
– the systems and processes in your work place they will be interested in.

3 Now act out the visit. Decide who should be the host and the visitor in the scenario you created.

The host should begin by welcoming the visitor. Don't forget to start with some friendly conversation before you get down to business.

CHECK OUT

1 In this unit you have practised hosting a visit from foreign business contacts. Have you completed all the tasks? Look back at the unit aims on page 16 and tick (✓) the tasks you have done.
2 Which tasks did you find most useful? Why?
3 Which tasks did you find most difficult? Why?
4 Are there tasks you need to study further?

MAKE A NOTE OF
• useful things you want to remember
• difficult things you want to study further

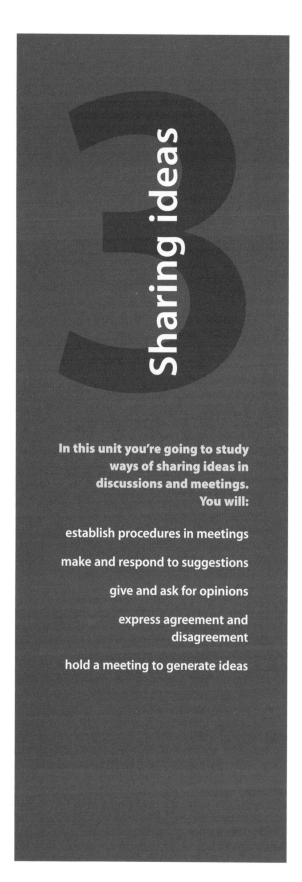

3 Sharing ideas

In this unit you're going to study ways of sharing ideas in discussions and meetings. You will:

establish procedures in meetings

make and respond to suggestions

give and ask for opinions

express agreement and disagreement

hold a meeting to generate ideas

▶ MEETINGS

1 What different kinds of meeting do you go to? Do you ever have meetings to brainstorm ideas at your company? How are they different from other meetings?

2 Read about a brainstorming meeting at Mattel, the producer of the famous Barbie doll. How is it similar to or different from the meetings you attend?

THE MEETING THEY HATE TO MISS

MATTEL IS FAMOUS FOR INNOVATIVE NEW TOYS, SO WHEN THEY START BRAINSTORMING IDEAS, IT'S A MEETING NO ONE LIKES TO MISS.

PARTICIPANTS Company executives, producers, and a facilitator **FREQUENCY** Monthly **PURPOSE** To come up with ideas for new products (and have fun!) **LOCATION** A comfortable hotel room with couches and computers and a projection system **DRESS CODE** Casual **PROCEDURE** Every meeting has a single-theme agenda. The facilitator makes sure everybody gets a chance to speak, and that only one person speaks at a time. Nobody is allowed to criticize another person's ideas. The facilitator stands at the front of the room with a PC and uses a projector with Microsoft Word Outliner to type in the main ideas as everyone talks. Nobody else is allowed to take notes. Everyone laughs a lot and when they get tired and unproductive, they play a quick game. Before the meeting breaks up, they put together a list of who's going to do what and by when; then everyone goes off to work on their assignments. **ENERGY SOURCE** Coffee, fruit, and bagels – soda and cookies in the afternoon.

KEY VOCABULARY

an agenda a list of things to discuss at a meeting
an assignment a task, a job
CEO Chief Executive Officer
to chair a meeting to run or control a meeting
to come up with to find or produce an answer
a facilitator someone who helps to makes things happen more easily
general counsel a position usually held by someone with legal training
innovative using new and clever ideas
the minutes the written record of what was said at a meeting
a strategy a plan you use in order to achieve something
unproductive not producing much

3 Think of questions to ask to get information about the meeting's participants, frequency, purpose, location, dress code, procedure, and energy source.

e.g. *Who goes to the meeting?*
 How often is the meeting held?

Compare your questions with a partner and check your ideas in File 1 on page 54.

4 Now find out about meetings in two other companies. Work with a partner. One person should use the information in File 4 on page 55. The other should use the information in File 10 on page 58.

Word combinations

When you're learning a new word, pay attention to the other words around it. Look for words that are often used together.

 For example, when a meeting starts, we ask someone to *take* the minutes, not to *write* the minutes. There's no special reason. People just usually say *take* with *minutes*. Similarly, we don't talk about *large* competition or *hard* competition. Instead, we say *strong* competition or *heavy* competition and it will sound strange if you say *large* or *hard*.

 So as well as learning single words, try to learn word combinations.

5 *Brainstorm, come up with, exchange,* and *criticize* are all verbs that we use with the noun *ideas*. Think of some different verbs that can be used in front of these nouns or noun phrases, e.g. to *chair* a meeting, to *hold* a meeting.

a   a meeting
b   an agenda
c   future strategy
d   advice
e   details
f   the minutes

6 Match the nouns a–f with a group of verbs 1–6.

1   have, follow, stick to, cover all the items on
2   take, read, check, keep
3   give, offer a piece of, take, ask for some
4   plan, discuss, implement, decide on
5   chair, hold, cancel, do your homework before
6   go into, note down, ask for, need more

Output task

1 Prepare to talk about the meetings you attend. Make brief notes on the following:

– participants
– frequency
– purpose
– procedure
– location
– dress code
– energy source
– things you like and
  dislike about them.

2 Work with a partner. Take it in turns to ask and answer questions about the meetings you attend. Remember to find out what your partner likes and dislikes about their meetings.

▶ SUGGESTIONS

1 Some products are sold with 'free' gifts that make consumers want to buy them. Can you think of any examples? What kinds of products are sold with free gifts to attract children?

2 [3.1] A marketing team is looking at a model of a plastic toy that they're planning to put in breakfast cereal boxes. Listen and find out what kind of toy it is.

3 Can you remember the decisions the marketing team made? Which of the following things are they going to do?

a   make the toy in different colours
b   do some market research to find out what colours are best
c   make the eyes bigger
d   make a different toy for girls
e   put a noise-maker in the bottom
f   give the alien some clothes

   [3.1] Listen again and check your answers.

4 [3.1] The speakers used different expressions to make suggestions. Listen again and fill in the missing words.

1   .... do some market research to find out.

2   .... just choose three or four bright colours, then?

3   .... the eyes bigger?

4   .... a different toy for girls?

5   .... a noise-maker in the bottom?

6   And .... give it something extra.

Suggestions

There are several different ways of making suggestions.

We could *do some research.*
Why don't we *do some research?*
Couldn't we *do some research?*

Notice that the verb changes to an *–ing* form if we say *How about …?* and *What about …?*

How about *doing some research?*
What about *doing some research?*

To make a suggestion stronger, we can say:

I think we should *do some market research.*

KEY VOCABULARY

an alien a creature from another planet
bright colours strong colours
can't afford unable to buy something because you do

not have enough money
kids *(informal)* children
to look into to investigate
a price estimate a written statement giving a price for doing a job

5 Here are the expressions the team used to respond to suggestions. Next to each expression, note if:

it is a positive response (+)
it is a negative response (–)
it suggests investigation (?)

a   Good idea.   ....
b   It's worth investigating.   ....
c   It'll take too long.   ....
d   That's a great idea.   ....
e   It isn't worth it.   ....
f   I think we should look into it. ....
g   We can't afford it.   ....
h   That'll work.   ....
i   OK, let's check it out.   ....
j   It's too complicated.   ....

Output task

Work in small groups. Your company produces breakfast cereal and you want to include small gifts in the box to attract young consumers. You need to think of ideas for gifts that your company can use for market research.

1 First think about your target market. What ages are the children? What interests do they have?

2 Now brainstorm ideas for as many different gifts and toys as you can.

3 Choose the best idea and work out some details.

–   What size is it?
–   What colour(s) is it?
–   What's it made of?
–   Are you going to pack it? (If so, how?)

4 Draw a picture or diagram of the gift. When you've finished, present your idea to the class. See if they can suggest improvements.

▶ OPINIONS

1 Do you belong to a political party? Have you ever taken part in local politics? Would you like to be a politician? Why/Why not?

2 Read this political literature. Would you vote for Eileen MacCaul?

KEY VOCABULARY

a fine a sum of money that you have to pay if you break the law

to pollute to make the air, rivers, etc. dirty and dangerous

sustainable able to keep going without running out – wind and solar power are 'sustainable sources of energy'

to vote to express your choice in an election

If you think

- everyone should be able to breathe clean air ✔
- companies that pollute should pay heavy fines ✔
- we need more investment in sustainable sources of energy ✔
- our environment is too important to be left to the free market ✔
- there should be more government controls on private businesses ✔

Vote Eileen MacCaul on May 8th

Opinions

We often use the verb *think* to express and ask for opinions in English.

I think *pollution is a serious problem.*
I don't think *I'd vote for Eileen MacCaul.*
What do you think about *sustainable sources of energy?*

We can also use *should* and *shouldn't* to talk about what is right, correct, or proper.

I think companies that pollute **should** *pay heavy fines.*
I don't think we **should** *leave this to the free market.*
Do you think there **should** *be more government controls?*

3 Ask a partner if they agree with each of Eileen MacCaul's views.

A *Do you think everyone should be able to breathe clean air?*
B *Yes, I do. / No, I don't.*
A *I agree. / I disagree.*

QUICK CHECK

Look at these sentences. Which ones are correct English and which ones are wrong?

1 *You're right.*
2 *You have right.*
3 *I am agree.*
4 *Are we all agreed?*
5 *Are you agree?*
6 *Do you agree?*

4 Read what Adam Smith, the eighteenth-century economist, thought about governments and free markets. Do you think his ideas are still relevant today?

Smith

Smith Adam born Kirkcaldy, Scotland, June 5, 1723 died July 17, 1790. Social philosopher and economist.

Many people regard Adam Smith as the founder of modern economics. In his famous book, The Wealth of Nations, Smith said that governments should not interfere with their countries' economic systems. He felt that the best way to achieve economic growth was through private efforts, not public ones. So he was against state controls on private businesses and against state-owned companies.

But this doesn't mean that Smith trusted business people more than politicians. In fact, he didn't trust business people at all. He said that they are motivated by self-interest and that whenever they meet together, they start looking for ways to raise prices. But Smith believed in competition and a free market. He looked at how economic systems develop over time and argued that competition leads businesses to supply the goods consumers want, both cheaply and efficiently.

Smith didn't think governments should interfere in international trade and he disagreed strongly with tariffs and trade barriers. He believed that free trade increased the wealth of nations.

KEY VOCABULARY

economics the study of the way money, trade, and industry are organized
to interfere to take part in someone else's affairs when your help isn't wanted or needed
to raise to increase
self-interest concern for what is best for yourself, rather than for other people
state controls ways that a government limits and controls something
a tariff a tax on imports
a trade barrier something that stops trade or makes it difficult

5 Match the phrases a–e with another phrase 1–5 to make sentences about Adam Smith's views.

a He thought
b He believed in
c He was against
d He didn't trust
e He didn't think

1 governments should interfere with private business.
2 politicians or business people.
3 free trade and competition.
4 governments shouldn't interfere with international trade.
5 tariffs and trade barriers.

Do you think Adam Smith was right?

Output task

1 In many parts of the world, neighbouring governments have formed free trade associations like ASEAN, NAFTA, MERCOSUR, and the EU. Is your country a member of such an association? Are any other countries applying for membership? What are the advantages and disadvantages of belonging?

2 Prepare to exchange your opinions on free trade agreements. First, think about the links between your country and its neighbours. How close should they be? Do you agree or disagree with these statements?

a There should be no trade barriers or tariffs.
b We should have the same laws for the sale and distribution of goods.
c We should be able to move freely between one country and another.
d There should be a shared army.
e There should be a shared health service.
f We should have the same education system.
g We should have the same currency.

3 When you're ready, work in small groups and compare your opinions.

▶ AGREEING AND DISAGREEING

1 Are your company's prices generally higher or lower than its competitors' prices? When people are setting prices in your industry, which of these factors are important?

- the prices charged by your competitors
- the prices charged by the company in other countries or markets
- production costs
- distribution costs
- currency fluctuations
- strategic goals, e.g. whether you want market share or a quick profit
- something else (what?)

2 ⌊3.2⌋ ⌊3.3⌋ ⌊3.4⌋ A product manager is deciding how to price a new product. Listen to her talking to three different colleagues. Which factor does each colleague think is important?

3 ⌊3.2⌋ ⌊3.3⌋ ⌊3.4⌋ Listen to the conversations again. Do the speakers agree or disagree with each other? What section of the company do you think the three colleagues might work in? Whose advice do you think is most useful, and why?

4 ⌊3.2⌋ Listen to the first conversation again and find examples of people saying *Yes, but …* when they disagree.

5 ⌊3.3⌋ Listen to the second conversation and find more tentative expressions of these ideas.

a We don't have to do that.
b That's not true!
c But we'll make less profit.

KEY VOCABULARY

a bill a written request for payment, an invoice
to charge *(a price)* to ask customers to pay a particular amount of money
a feature an important or interesting part of something
in the long run over a long period of time in the future

a margin an amount of profit that a company makes on something
a market strategy a plan you use to improve your position in a market
running costs money you need to spend to operate a business

6 ⌊3.4⌋ Listen to the third conversation again and find examples of rephrasing.

Agreeing and disagreeing

When we disagree, we often soften what we are saying. So instead of saying *No!* we might say *Yes, but …* and then add our reservations.

We sometimes sound tentative, too. So instead of saying *You're wrong!* we might say *I think you might be wrong*, or *I'm not sure if you're right*. Sounding tentative like this can be more polite, especially in British English.

When we agree, we often rephrase, saying the same thing again but using different words.

A *It'll reduce our customers' energy bills.*
B *Exactly. They'll spend a lot less on electricity.*

Output task

Price isn't the only factor that's important when we're buying something. Think about your clients and customers. Apart from price, what other things are important for them?

1 Look at this list and rank the factors in order of priority. (Write 1 for the most important factor and 6 for the least important.)

- ☐ low prices and attractive credit terms
- ☐ a product or supplier with a good reputation
- ☐ reliability – a product / supplier you can trust
- ☐ good guarantees and after-sales service
- ☐ helpful and efficient sales staff
- ☐ something else (what?)

2 Compare your answers with a partner. Try to agree on a combined ranking.

▶ HOLDING A MEETING

1 Look at the photographs. Does your town or city have similar problems to these? Do you know any more cities with serious traffic problems? What solutions can you think of?

2 Work with a partner. One person should turn to File 12 on page 59. The other should turn to File 15 on page 60.

A The traffic in Bangkok is so bad that around three hundred babies are born in cars on their way to the hospital each year. Many traffic police take a course in midwifery.

B One in fifty heart attack victims arriving at London hospitals are there because of polluted air. London traffic moves at the same average speed today as it did a hundred years ago – just 17 km per hour.

C Motorists in some Italian cities spend between thirty minutes and an hour each day looking for a parking space. That adds up to two years of an average lifetime.

Output task

Work in small groups. You're responsible for improving traffic conditions in your home town or city. Hold a meeting to decide how to improve the flow of traffic, ease parking problems, and reduce pollution. Each person at the meeting should make a suggestion. You can use the ideas in 2 above or use your own ideas.

1 As a group, decide on the procedure for the meeting.

– Will you have a chairperson or facilitator? (If so, who?)
– Who will take notes of your ideas, and how? (white board, overhead projector, note pad?)
– Will you brainstorm ideas first and then evaluate them, or evaluate them as you go along?
– In what order will you speak?

2 Individually, prepare what you're going to say. Then start the meeting. Discuss everyone's ideas and decide which ones are best.

4 Exchanging information

In this unit you are going to study communication strategies that will help you exchange information accurately and effectively. You will:

get your meaning across when you don't know what to say

check that you have understood what was said

provide an information update

collect information about a business problem

conduct research into products and suppliers

▶ EXPLANATIONS

1 [4.1] Look at the photographs. What do you think the product is? What is it for? Listen to someone describing it and complete the specifications table.

BOB SPECIFICATIONS

Dimensions	H 132cm x W 68cm x L 94cm
Maximum speed	
Maximum depth	
Average dive time	
Battery	
Price	

2 [4.1] Listen again. How does the woman get the information she wants? Note down the questions she asks.

3 [4.1] Listen again. How does the man describe what BOB is like? Fill in the missing phrases.

a .... a jet-ski – it travels under the water instead of on top.
b .... explore shipwrecks, study fish, whatever you want, really.
c So, ... a submarine.
d Yes, ... a one-person submarine.
e .... dive down under the sea.
f .... a space suit.
g .... dives of about fifty minutes.
h .... a small electric motor.
i .... a rechargeable 12-volt battery.

4 Work with a partner to complete this crossword. One person should use the crossword on the right. The other should use the crossword in File 5 on page 55.

A There are no clues to this crossword. Your partner has the words you need, and you have the words your partner needs. You can't say the missing words, but make up clues to help your partner:

Two across: You use it to add up figures.
Six down: It's made of plastic and ...

CALCULATOR
CARD
ADDRESS
CALENDAR
DICTIONARY
LIGHT
PRICE
CLOCK
TABLE
PAPER
MIRROR
TRAIN
YEN
ADVERTISEMENT

Output task

File 7

The Wave Monofin

File 17

The Street-Wiz Scooter

File 11

The Space Suit

Work in groups of two or three. Each person is going to find out about a product and describe it to the group. Other group members can ask any questions they like, e.g. What's it made of? What's it for? How big is it?

1 Look at the pictures above and choose one product each. Then turn to the appropriate files to learn more about them.

2 When you are ready, take it in turns to describe your product and answer questions about it. You can invent any information you don't know.

QUICK CHECK

1 [4.2] Can you pronounce the alphabet in English? Say it aloud. Check your pronunciation with your teacher or compare it with the recording.

2 Which letters are pronounced differently in your language? Can you think of ways to remember the different pronunciations?

3 Spell your name, company name, and address.

▶ CHECKING INFORMATION

1 ⟨4.3⟩ Listen to some people double checking information on the phone. Is the information below right or wrong? Correct any mistakes.

a   976824
b   20 x H396, 30 x G642
c $30
d   3.30, 16 March
e   send more information

2 Listen again and note down the phrases used to check what was said.

Checking

We can check information in different ways. We can ask people to repeat what they said.

Sorry?
Could you say that again?
I didn't catch that.

Or we can repeat what they said ourselves.

The sixth?   *Did you say ...?*

We can also repeat what they said using different words.

So you mean ...?
Could we run through that again? So it's ...

We can say *so* and *then* when we want confirmation.

***So** it's not a good price, **then**.*
   No, it isn't.
***So,** see you on the sixth at three thirty, **then**.*
   Yes, see you on the sixth.

To correct someone, we often stress the information that is different.

Reference number G 642.
No, J 642.

Output task

Work with a partner. Make telephone calls to check information. One person should look at the information below. The other should look at the information in File 6 on page 56.

You are Val Charvet.

1   Someone took this phone message for you yesterday. Read through it. Does anything look strange? Phone Jan Hendrikssen and check the information. Correct any mistakes.

> *Message from Jan*
> *Hendrikssen*
> *– 31 20 367 898*
>
> *Jan is arriving at 22.10 on*
> *Tuesday morning with 14*
> *delegates from the German*
> *Class Makers Federation.*

2   You left a message yesterday for one of your colleagues, who was out of the office when you called them. Your colleague is going to call you to check the information they received. This is the message you left.

> *Could you arrange a meeting*
> *with Jay E. Stein in order to*
> *set deadlines and discuss the*
> *oil leakages?*

▶ UPDATING

1 What do you do when you call someone and they're not at their desk? Do you often leave or receive voicemail messages?

2 [4.4] Listen to someone leaving a voicemail message and answer these questions.

a What type of video is Seth going to make?
b What has he done so far?
c What does he need Carmen to do?

3 [4.5] Listen to Carmen's reply. What's the problem?

4 [4.6] Listen to Seth's reply. Who's going to use the video? Why can't he film in Denver?

5 [4.7] Listen to Carmen's reply. What exactly does she ask Seth to do?

6 [4.8] Listen to the next message. What questions does Carmen ask?

7 [4.9] Here's Seth's list of jobs. Listen to his message and tick (✓) the things he's done so far.

> *To do*
>
> Speak with Chuck and set a date – 215 555 7693
> Hire a camera operator
> Book flights to Philadelphia
> Rent equipment
> Hire African-American and Asian actors
> Do a new budget
> Show it to Carmen and get authorization
> Update Carmen on progress

KEY VOCABULARY

to authorize to give official permission, usually in writing
to get in touch with to write to, phone, or email someone
to set a date to decide on a date

to sign to write your name on a document
tied up busy
to update / to bring someone up to date to give someone current news about progress

Present perfect

We use the Present perfect to talk about past actions that are still important. We often use it to give news and talk about recent activities.

I've spoken to Chuck in Philadelphia.
I haven't rented the equipment yet.

Notice that the time reference here is indefinite. If there's a definite time reference, we usually use the Simple past instead.

Sorry I didn't call yesterday.

We form the Present perfect with *have* + the past participle of the main verb. In regular verbs the past participle and past tense forms are the same. But with irregular verbs, they may be different.

I spoke to Chuck yesterday. (past tense form)
I've spoken to Chuck in Philadelphia. (past participle form)

8 Work with a partner. Look at Seth's 'to do' list in 7. Ask and answer questions about his progress.

Has he spoken to Chuck yet?
> *Yes, he has and they've set a date.*

Output task

1 How is your work going? Prepare to update someone on your progress. Think of either a project you're involved in at the moment, or all the things you're doing this week. Write a list of tasks. Include all the tasks you have done so far and tasks you haven't done yet.

2 Work with a partner. Use your lists to tell one another what you're doing and how much progress you've made.

▶ GETTING THE FACTS

1 `4.10` Listen to this telephone call. What's the problem and what do they decide to do about it?

2 `4.10` Listen again. What questions and phrases does Vic use to do these things?

a find out what's wrong
b check she understands the problem
c find out what's been done so far
d promise action
e check Chris has nothing else to say

3 `4.10` Notice Chris's intonation when he says: *Then why aren't they here?* Does he sound puzzled or angry?

4 `4.11` Listen to some people saying these expressions in two different ways. Each time do they sound angry and aggressive, or friendly but puzzled?
1 *Then why aren't they here?*
2 *Then where are they?*
3 *Well, we don't have them.*
4 *Well, they never made it here.*

5 Practise saying the phrases in two different ways. The first time, try to sound angry and aggressive. The second time, try to sound friendly but puzzled.

6 `4.10` Listen to the conversation again and follow it on the chart on page 41. Then read the conversation with a partner. Use the chart to make more conversations. Follow the arrows and make as many different conversations as you can. Try to use all the squares. Remember to sound polite, not aggressive.

7 Look at the chart again and find all the expressions the callers use to:

a request help
b offer help
c promise action.

8 Work with a partner. Close your books and act out similar calls.

QUICK CHECK

Can you understand what people are saying to you on the phone? Check your telephone English with these questions.

1 Someone says these things to you on the phone. What's your reply?
  a *Who's calling, please?*
  b *Will you hold?*
  c *I'm afraid the line's busy.*
  d *I'll put you through.*
  e *I'm afraid Mr Azzaro isn't in today.*
  f *Can you call me back?*
  g *Was there anything else?*

2 To ask us to wait, someone might say:
  One moment, please.
  What else could they say?

3 Ask someone these questions and write down the answers.
  Can I have your telephone number?
  And your area code?
  And do you have an extension number?

4 The recorded message says 'Press the pound key'. Which button do you press?

a ✳   b #

Output task

Work with a partner. One person should use the information below and the other should use the information in File 3 on page 54.

You export frozen chickens and turkeys. You send them by sea in refrigerated containers. A customer in South Africa calls you with a problem.

1 Find out what the problem is.
2 Find out what's been done so far.
3 Decide what to do and promise action.

START HERE

Hi, Vic. It's Chris.	Vic Santoro.	Vic Santoro, please.	Hello, Platinum Systems.	No, it's all right thanks. It can wait.	OK.	Thanks. Bye.
Hello, Chris. What can I do for you?	Chris Frantz from Marketing in Austria.	Who's calling, please?	Could I speak to Vic Santoro?	I'm afraid Vic's not in today. Do you want to leave a message?	When's she back?	Tomorrow.
We've got a problem.	What's up?	It's the leaflets for the exhibition. They're not here.	That's the shipment for Vienna?	Yes, it's 805-974.	Do you have the shipment number?	Ah, I can't wait that long. Do you work with Vic?
The delivery address was Hubertus-damm?	No, and the exhibition opens on Monday.	You mean they haven't arrived in Vienna yet?	Yes, that's the one.	OK, one moment. I'm running a search.	No, can you find out if Vic's sent them?	Yes. I'm her colleague, Toshi Kamara.
Yes, the Austria Center exhibition centre.	That's strange. They were sent last Wednesday.	Well, we don't have them.	I'm looking for the shipping form now. Yes, got it. We sent 3,000.	Thanks.	And they haven't arrived?	I'm Chris Frantz and I work in marketing in the Austrian office.
According to our records, they were dispatched on the 8th.	Then why aren't they here?	Somebody signed for them. I have a name here … Jean-Pierre Marceau.	Well, they never made it here.	OK, according to our computer, they were delivered last Wednesday.	Vic was supposed to send me some leaflets for an exhibition that opens here next week.	And how can I help you, Chris?
Then where are they?	Have you contacted the freight company?	But he works in Paris, not Vienna.	Perhaps they've gone to the wrong country.	Oh no!	Would you like me to look into it and try to track them down?	Yes, please.
OK. I'll call them and find out what's happened.	No, I thought it was your responsibility.	Yes, I have it here. Was there anything else?	No, that's all thanks. I'll wait to hear from you, then.	I'll see what I can do. Is that it, or was there another problem?	Good, we need them for Monday.	OK. I'll do my best.
Thanks. Could you do it right away?	Sure, I'll call you back as soon as I have any information.	Do you know my extension number?	Yes, sure.	Thanks a lot. Bye.	Yes, I'll get back to you as soon as I can.	Thanks, and could you keep me informed?

▶ DOING RESEARCH

1 How do you get the equipment and supplies you need at work? Does your organization have a Purchasing Department? Who authorizes your purchases? What documents do you use?

2 Look quickly at this catalogue information for Salem Glass. What does the company manufacture? Who do you think buys their products?

3 Look at the catalogue again. What changes has the company introduced in its product range this year?
e.g. *It's introduced more sizes of the immersion tubes.*

Salem Glass

Customers may deduct 10% if they pay within 15 days of invoice.

Immersion Tubes *out of stoc*

Ref No.	1/10	1/20	1/30	1/60	1/80
Diameter	10 mm	20 mm	30 mm	60 mm	80 mm
Length	110 mm	110 mm	180 mm	180 mm	180 m
Price	$15.53	$17.08	$18.10	$35.72	$45.05

Sulfur Absorption Tubes

Ref No.	SA/110
Diameter Top	30 mm
Capacity	130 ml
Price	$21.60

Hirsh Funnels

Ref No.	J/147	G/147
Tube Diameter	20 mm	30 mm
Top Diameter	50 mm	75 mm
Price	$21.22	$24.46

Bubblers

Ref No.	B/1
Tube Length	100 mm
Capacity	20 ml
Price	$36.42

Gooch Crucibles

Ref No.	GC/30	GC/40
Diameter	30 mm	40 mm
Height	60 mm	60 mm
Price	$17.70	$21.70

Environmentally Friendly

We are pleased to announce that we are now using recycled glass in all our products.

News Flash

All designs now approved by the Environmental Protection Agency.

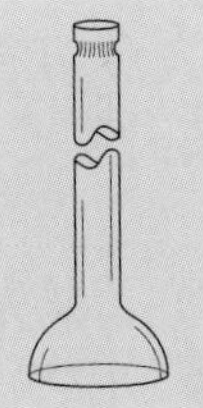

Now available in more sizes!

Now available in unbreakable glass!

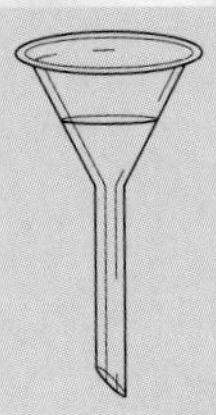

New low price!

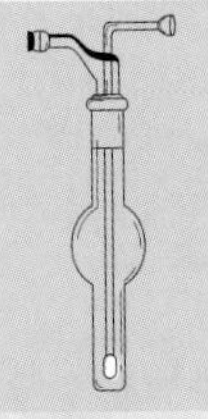

New line!

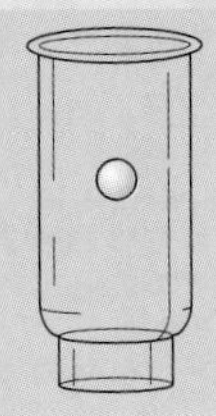

Modified design allows easier cleaning!

Output task

Work with a partner. One person should use the information on this page. The other should use the information in File 14 on page 60.

You work for Salem Glass. Take a call from a customer. Use the information in your catalogue to answer their questions. Make a note of their details and the items they plan to order. Be careful – there are some problems to solve.

File 14 on page 60.

CHECK OUT

1   In this unit you have studied communication strategies that will help you exchange information accurately and effectively. Have you completed all the tasks? Look back at the unit aims on page 36 and tick (✓) the tasks you have done.
2   Which tasks did you find most useful? Why?
3   Which tasks did you find most difficult? Why?
4   Are there tasks you need to study further?

MAKE A NOTE OF
• useful things you want to remember
• difficult things you want to study further

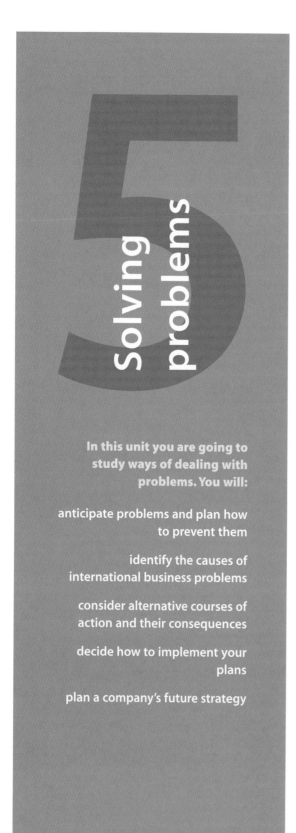

Solving problems

In this unit you are going to study ways of dealing with problems. You will:

anticipate problems and plan how to prevent them

identify the causes of international business problems

consider alternative courses of action and their consequences

decide how to implement your plans

plan a company's future strategy

▶ ANTICIPATING PROBLEMS

1 Does demand for your company's products or services remain steady throughout the year, or does it change? Why? What problems do seasonal changes in demand cause you?

2 Read what happens at Nintendo and predict the seasonal demand problem they will have. Answer the questions below.

Nintendo manufactures computer games systems and it operates a telephone helpdesk for its customers. If they need help setting up their computer system and playing the games, they can call the company's helplines and a technical advisor will answer their questions.

a In what month of the year will Nintendo make most of its sales?
b What will happen to the helpdesk in the week after Christmas?
c Can you suggest any solutions to this problem?

Making predictions, *will*

We use *will* to make predictions about the future.

*Nintendo **will** make most of its sales in December.*

Will is often contracted to *'ll*.

*It'**ll** receive thousands of calls in the week after Christmas.*

The negative form is *will not*. It's usually contracted to *won't*.

*There **won't** be enough technical employees to answer all the questions.*

WOW, IT'S WORKING!

In the week after Christmas, Nintendo receives around half a million telephone calls from customers across North America. Most come from adults who have bought new sets for their children and can't get them to work. But with up to 125,000 calls a day, there simply aren't enough people to operate the phones. This year, however, Nintendo has found a novel solution. The company is employing high school students like Katie Shaughnessy to take the calls and tell the adults what to do.

'Ma'am, I'd like you to try setting it to channel two', says sixteen-year-old Katie. 'Now do you see where it says 'input' on your remote control? Press that. Anything? No? OK, press it again.' A pause at the other end of the line. 'Wait! Hey, there it is!' the woman exclaims. 'Wow, it's working! Thanks!'

Nintendo has another satisfied customer.

KEY VOCABULARY

to exclaim to say something suddenly because you're surprised

novel unusual

a remote control a device for operating electronic equipment from a distance

3 Read this opening part of an article. How is Nintendo dealing with the problem?

4 Discuss these questions.

a What are the advantages and disadvantages of this solution?
b What kind of training will the high school students need to do this job?
c What would you pay the students per hour to do this job?
d Would you pay them the same as the full-time helpdesk employees?
e Would you provide other benefits? If so, what?

5 Work with a partner and read some more of the article. One person should look at File 13 on page 59. The other should look at File 18 on page 61. Find out what else happens at Nintendo and exchange information with your partner.

6 Discuss these questions with some other students.

a Is Nintendo's solution to the Christmas helpdesk problem a good one?
b Would it work in your country?
c What kinds of problems could there be? (Think about trade unions, employment laws, public opinion.)

Output task

What problems will your company or department face in the future? Discuss these questions with a partner.

1 Will your workload remain steady or will it change? What problems will this cause and how will you deal with them?
2 Will you need more or fewer employees in the future? Why?
3 Will the employees in your department need more training in the future? What kind of training and why?
4 Can you predict any other problems that your company or department will face in the future? What are they and what will you do about them?

▶ IDENTIFYING CAUSES

1 Where does your company advertise its products and services? Some companies use the same advertisement to sell their products all over the world. Can you think of any examples? What are the advantages of global advertising? And what disadvantages might there be?

2 Look at this advertisement. What's it selling? If you translated it into your language, would it work in your country? Do you think it would work everywhere?

'BIG BOTTLES WITH BIG SAVINGS'

4
リットル

Brisk

食器洗い

* Attacks dirt and grease *
* Leaves dishes sparkling clean *
* Big savings on giant 4-litre bottles *

3 [5.1] A soap manufacturer is having problems selling this dish-washing liquid in Japan. Listen and find out what might have been causing the problem.

4 [5.1] Listen again. How do the speakers talk about the possible causes of the problem? Fill in the missing words.

a Well, the price .... the problem. It's very competitive.

b .... we've priced it too low.

c Well, it .... that people equate price with quality.

d It .... the advertisement.

e .... it was because of that line about four-litre bottles.

f I'm not sure, but it .... because people read the pictures from bottom to top, instead of top to bottom.

Which sentences sound certain (C) and which sound uncertain (U)?

Making deductions

We use the modal verbs *must, can, might,* and *could* to make deductions. When we're certain, we use *must be* in positive sentences and *can't be* in negative sentences.

*I know it **can't be** the price that's the problem. It **must be** something else.*

When we're less certain, we use *could be* and *might be.*

*I'm not sure. The problem **could be** the size, or it **might be** the low price.*

To make deductions about past situations, we use the Present perfect forms.

*It **can't have been** the translation so it **must have been** the pictures.*
*It **could have been** because people read from bottom to top, or it **might have been** because the bottle was too big.*

Output task

1 Work with a partner. Read some true stories about some international business problems. Can you work out what caused them? Make deductions with *must have been*, *can't have been*, *could have been*, and *might have been*. When you have finished, check your answers in File 9 on page 57.

2 Have you ever had, or have you ever heard about, any similar problems to these? What cultural problems has your company had operating in different countries? Explain the problems to some other students.

A	The magazine *Time* is published all over the world. In its Brazilian edition, it ran an advertisement in Spanish but the ad failed to attract new customers. Why?
B	An American supermarket wanted to impress some Japanese visitors so they cooked some sushi (a traditional Japanese fish dish) to serve to their guests. The guests were not pleased. Why not?
C	When United Airlines started flying from Hong Kong, they gave all their passengers a white carnation as a complimentary gift. A lot of passengers didn't want to accept the gift. Why not?
D	A glass company in Taiwan packed their products in hay (dried grass) to protect them for transport. Their products usually travelled well, but when they sent some glasses to the Middle East, they all arrived broken. Why?
E	McDonald's, the fast food company, ran a special promotion at the 1984 Olympic Games in Los Angeles. They awarded customers with prizes whenever a US athlete won a medal. The problem was they miscalculated and the promotion cost a lot more than they budgeted for. Why did they miscalculate?
F	General Motors had difficulty introducing a new Chevrolet car called the Nova in Puerto Rico. The car didn't sell until they changed the name. Why?

▶ CONSIDERING ALTERNATIVES

1 What different types of software does your company use to perform its business activities? Are there any problems with it? Does it have software that integrates different activities like purchasing, manufacturing, logistics, etc.?

2 〔5.2〕 Listen to some managers discussing the possibility of buying some business software. Is their company going to buy it?

3 〔5.2〕 Listen again. Make brief notes of the advantages and disadvantages of buying the software in the boxes below. Do you think the company should buy the software?

Buying the software
advantages
disadvantages

Not buying the software
advantages
disadvantages

KEY VOCABULARY

to adapt to change your behaviour because the situation you're in has changed

a competitive edge the things you have or do give you an advantage over your competitors

to integrate to combine, to join things together

out of business no longer trading, bankrupt

to recoup an initial investment to get back money that was invested at the start of a project

to re-engineer to completely change the way all the business activities of an organization are structured

tool a piece of equipment or software that helps you do a job

---

if- sentences

We use *if* to talk about things that might happen.

If we buy this software … (perhaps we'll buy it, perhaps we won't.)

We often use *if* when we are considering alternative courses of action.

If we buy this software …
If we don't buy this software …

Notice we don't use *will* in the same clause as *if*.

~~*If we will buy this software*~~, *it will take a year to implement.*

Instead we use the present tense to express a future idea.

*If we **buy** this software, it will take a year to implement.*

4 〔5.2〕 Match the first parts of each sentence a–f with the second parts 1–6. Then listen again and check your answers.

a   If it works,
b   If we go ahead and buy it,
c   So what happens if
d   So, if we don't buy it,
e   If the implementation process goes smoothly,
f   But if it takes take too long,

1   we don't buy the software?
2   it could put us out of business.
3   we'll recoup our initial investment in three years.
4   we might lose our competitive edge.
5   we'll have to re-engineer the whole company.
6   it'll be fantastic.

Output task

Work with a partner. Decide what to do in these situations. First say what your alternatives are. Then consider the advantages and disadvantages of each one.

1   Your competitor has launched a rival product. Their price is 10% lower than yours. Should you respond by cutting your price or not?

3   You're redesigning your headquarters. The architect wants to know if you'd like an open plan office with no walls or lots of small rooms and corridors. Which alternative is best?

4   You have two excellent candidates for the job of Sales Manager. One has worked with your company for twenty years and knows a lot about your products and services. The other one is younger and has worked for your major competitor. Who should you employ?

5   Many of your office employees want to telecommute and do their jobs from home using computers and modems. Should you agree or not?

2   The launch of your new software product is scheduled for next month but it still has a lot of bugs. It isn't going to be ready but you know your competitors are launching a similar product very soon. Should you delay the launch or not?

▶ IMPLEMENTING

1 What do you like about your work? Everyone has jobs they like and don't like. What jobs do you enjoy doing and what jobs do you dislike?

2 ⟨5.3⟩ Listen to a project team discussing who's going to do a job. What job is it, and is it popular?

3 ⟨5.3⟩ Listen again and answer these questions.

a   Why do they need to fill out more time sheets?
b   Why can't Christophe do this job?
c   Why can't Isabelle do it either?
d   What exactly must Paul do?
e   What's Paul doing this week?
f   When's Paul going to do the work?
g   When must he do it by?

4 ⟨5.3⟩ Here are some of the expressions the people used to schedule the work. Try to remember the missing words, then listen again and check your answers.

a   That'll take .... two days.
b   Who is going to be .... this?
c   .... you do it, Paul?
d   How long .... it .... you?
e   .... send you my files.
f   You're good .... progress reports, Paul, so maybe you can do that too?
g   How .... can you do it?
h   Can you do it .... Friday?

Which phrases are used to:
a   decide who will do a job?
b   plan the schedule?

KEY VOCABULARY

behind schedule
doing things later than the time you planned

a bookkeeper
someone who keeps records of the money a business spends or receives

a deadline
a time or date before which work must be done

time sheets
documents that show how much time workers have spent on particular tasks

QUICK CHECK

Can you talk about schedules? Check and see.

1 We say we're *behind schedule* if we're doing things later than planned. What do we say if were doing things:

   a earlier than planned?

   b at the time we planned?

2 What's the difference between being *on time* and *in time*?

3 If someone says 'I can do the report by Friday', what do they mean?

   a I won't do it until Friday.

   b I'll do it on Friday.

   c It'll be ready on Friday.

5 Number these sentences in the correct order to make a short conversation. The first one has been done for you.

☐ I'm about halfway through.

☐ Not without working overtime.

[1] Who's responsible for preparing the production report?

☐ At least a week. I'm afraid I'm very tied up.

☐ How far have you got with it?

☐ Is that all? How long will it take to finish?

☐ Me, but I'm afraid I'm behind schedule.

☐ That's too long. Can't you do it by Friday?

Read the conversation with a partner. Then make up a similar one about a project plan.

Output task

1 Your company has decided to open a small gym for its employees to use during their breaks and free time. These are some of the jobs that need to be done. Read them through and decide which jobs you would be good at. Which jobs would you enjoy and which would you dislike?

> a Pass on information about the gym to all the employees.
>
> b Clear 1,500 boxes of old papers and files out of the room where the gym will be.
>
> c Organize a fund-raising event to contribute towards the costs of the gym.
>
> d Hire a part-time fitness coach and trainer.
>
> e Try out all the exercise equipment to make sure it works.
>
> f Arrange the visit of a famous sports personality to open the gym.
>
> g Keep the financial records and make sure all these jobs are done on time and within budget.

2 Now work in small groups. You are the committee responsible for setting up the gym. Go through the jobs one by one and decide who is going to do each one and when by. (Try to avoid the jobs you don't like and offer to do the jobs you like.)

▶ PLANNING STRATEGY

1 This is the in-tray of Jackie Halliday, the Financial Director of Hardine, a multinational pharmaceutical company. Look through the documents with a partner. Answer the questions and decide what Jackie should do about each one.

Memo
STRICTLY CONFIDENTIAL

Hardine Pharmaceuticals

From: Rod Lapinski, CEO
To: All members of the executive management
Re: Budget cuts

The fall in our revenues for the last three quarters requires firm action. All departments must cut back their budgets by 10% over the next twelve months. There will be no exceptions.

All department heads should prepare proposals for achieving these reductions. There will be a meeting of the executive board to discuss them tomorrow at 9.00 a.m. Please make sure you can attend.

RL

a What does Jackie need to do?
b What information about Hardine Pharmaceuticals would you like to have?
c Do you have any suggestions for how Jackie could make these cuts?

Thought you should see what the competition is doing.

Gretchen

$5 billion restructuring at Bellano

JOB CUTS FREE FUNDS FOR RESEARCH

Bellano, the multinational pharmaceutical group, today announced a major restructuring programme. The plans include reducing its workforce by 9% and selling additional shares to the public in order to finance research on new drugs.
'We've got a lot of exciting products in development,' said Jerry Harper, Bellano's CEO. 'This means we can focus our energies on bringing them to the market.' The announcement comes after a year of heavy competition from rival pharmaceutical companies such as Hardine and Frodol. Bellano claims that Valdura, their new arthritis drug currently under review from the Food and Drug Administration will be the

d What is Bellano?
e Do you think Bellano's share prices will rise or fall today? Why (not)?
f Does Jackie need to respond to this?

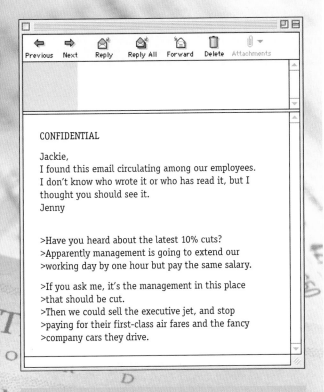

CONFIDENTIAL

Jackie,
I found this email circulating among our employees.
I don't know who wrote it or who has read it, but I
thought you should see it.
Jenny

>Have you heard about the latest 10% cuts?
>Apparently management is going to extend our
>working day by one hour but pay the same salary.

>If you ask me, it's the management in this place
>that should be cut.
>Then we could sell the executive jet, and stop
>paying for their first-class air fares and the fancy
>company cars they drive.

g Is this email a serious problem?
h What should Jackie do about it?

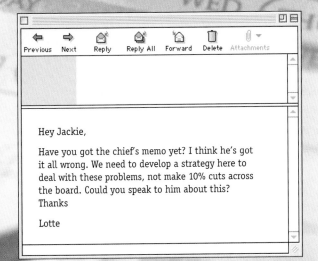

Hey Jackie,

Have you got the chief's memo yet? I think he's got
it all wrong. We need to develop a strategy here to
deal with these problems, not make 10% cuts across
the board. Could you speak to him about this?
Thanks

Lotte

i What does *across the board* mean?
j Who do you think Lotte is, and do you agree
   with her?
k Why isn't she talking to the CEO herself?
l How should Jackie respond?

2 ⏢5.4⏢ You are Jackie. You have just received a
voicemail message from the CEO. Listen and
make notes of what he wants you to do:

– before the meeting
– at the start of the meeting
– after the discussion of strategy
– before the meeting finishes.

3 Work with a partner. Look through the CEO's
draft proposals in File 8 on page 57 and make
sure you understand them all. Can you think of
any extra proposals to add?

Output task

1 Work in small groups. Prepare to hold the
meeting. First decide who is going to play the
role of Jackie Halliday and chair the meeting.
Then decide which sections of the company
everyone else is responsible for.

2 Plan what you will say at the meeting. Make
some brief notes, but don't write full sentences.
Just write key words. When you're ready, hold
the meeting and plan your strategy. Make sure
you agree on what to do about all the
proposals. Also decide what jobs needs to be
done, who will do them, and by when.

Information files

FILE 1

UNIT 3 Meetings 3, p29

There are several different ways to ask these questions. Compare your ideas with the questions below.

Participants
Who goes to the meeting?
Who attends the meeting?

Frequency
How often is the meeting held?
How frequently is the meeting held?

Purpose
What's the purpose of the meeting?
What's the meeting for?
Why do they hold the meeting?

Location
Where is the meeting held?
Where do they meet?

Dress code
What's the dress code?
What do people wear?
Do people wear suits and ties?

Procedure
What happens at the meeting?
What procedure does the meeting follow?

Energy source
What do people eat and drink?
What refreshments are served?

FILE 2

UNIT 2 Local information 2, p16

There are several different ways to ask the questions. Compare your suggestions with the questions below.

1   *What's the population of Beijing?*
    How many people live in Beijing?

2   *What's the official language of China?*
    What language do people speak in China?

3   *When do stores close in the evening?*
    What time do stores close?

4   *What are summers like?*
    What's the weather like in July and August?

5   *Who do you need to tip in some hotels?*
    Who should you tip?

6   *What kind of water should I drink?*
    Is it OK to drink the tap water?

FILE 3

UNIT 4 Getting the facts Output task, p40

You are in South Africa and you've ordered 250 cases of frozen chickens from your partner's company. A container with 250 cases of frozen turkeys has arrived, but no chickens. Call your partner. You want to know:

1   where your chickens are and when they will arrive
2   what to do with the turkeys.

Also, the turkey container must be kept at 17 degrees Celsius, so it's costing you money for electricity and storage. Find out who is going to pay for this. You have emailed the freight company but they haven't replied.

FILE 4

UNIT 3 Meetings 4, p29

You work for Yahoo!, the Internet services provider. Your partner works for Hannaford Bros, an American supermarket chain. Ask and answer questions to find out about meetings in each other's companies. Make brief notes in the table.

	Hannaford Bros	Yahoo!
Participants		The company founders, the CEO, senior managers, directors, and the general counsel.
Frequency		Monthly.
Purpose		To exchange ideas, talk about technology, and plan the company's future strategy.
Procedure		The CEO chairs the meeting and controls the pace, but the discussion is informal. They cover three or four major issues, but don't go into details.
Location		The main conference room at Yahoo!
Dress code		None – people wear what they like.
Energy source		Lots of caffeine and pizza.

FILE 5

UNIT 4 Explanations 4, p37

There are no clues to this crossword. Your partner has the words you need, and you have the words your partner needs. You can't say the missing words, but make up clues to help your partner like this:

One down: you use it to tell the time.
Sixteen across: they're made of steel and ...

WATCH
CAMERA
UMBRELLAS
OIL
DOLLAR
CH
HOUR
LIST
SCISSORS
BOTTLE
STORE
PEN
PHONE
CAR
IDEA
TIE

FILE 6

UNIT 4 Checking information Output task, p38

You are Jan Hendrikssen.

1 You left a message yesterday for one of your colleagues, who was out of the office when you called them. Your colleague is going to call you to check the information they received. This is the message you left.

> I am arriving at twenty to ten on Thursday morning, with forty delegates from the Dutch Glass Makers Federation.

2 Someone took this phone message for you yesterday. Read through it. Does anything look strange? Call Val Charvet and check it. Correct any mistakes.

Phone Message

From Val Charvet
Tel 33 1 46 57 11 00

Val wants you to arrange a meeting with J.I. Stein in order to sit death lines and discuss the oily cages.

FILE 7

UNIT 4 Explanations Output task, p37

KEY VOCABULARY

flexible easy to bend

to float to stay on the surface of liquid – opposite = *to sink*

a mermaid an imaginary sea creature, half-woman and half-fish

 File 7

The Wave is fast, fun, and designed for swimmers of all abilities. It works in a similar way to a mermaid's tail and enables you to swim more naturally through the water. It's a great way to improve swimming techniques and the perfect toy for the back-yard pool.

Available in blue or yellow, the Wave is 56 cm long and 45 cm wide. The blade is made of flexible polypropylene thermoplastic and the foot pockets are very soft, comfortable rubber. It only weighs one kilogram and it floats in water.

The Wave is designed to fit young swimmers and female feet and costs just $40. For sizes larger than US 81/2 there's a similar blade – the Rapid – which costs $80.

FILE 8

UNIT 5 Planning strategy 3, p53

DRAF PROPOSALS

MARKETING

Alternative 1
Purchase database software that will enable us to focus more sharply on market segments and target direct mail and advertising campaigns. The initial cost should be recouped over four years.

Alternative 2
Cut advertising by 50%.

FACILITIES MANAGEMENT

Alternative 1
Subcontract all maintenance, security, and transportation work.

Alternative 2
Cancel plans to redecorate the offices. Fire the gardener, throw out all the office plants and concrete over all the flower beds.

FINANCE

Alternative 1
Reduce shareholder dividends by 20%.

Alternative 2
Purchase software that integrates all the company's financial activities such as purchasing, manufacturing, customer order management, etc. We should recoup the initial investment in three years.

MANUFACTURING

Alternative 1
Subcontract the manufacture of smaller components and shut down one production line. This offers short-term savings, but will cost if we need to increase production again.

Alternative 2
Cut the third shift and make up lost production by increasing overtime on the other two shifts. (Production may fall slightly under current targets.)

INFORMATION TECHNOLOGY

Alternative 1
Cancel the plans to upgrade to a larger system with faster email, intranet and internet access, and reduce downtime for maintenance.

Alternative 2
Outsource programme development work and shift routine database maintenance work to remote servers in countries with lower labour costs.

RESEARCH AND DEVELOPMENT

Alternative 1
Cancel 20% of new product development projects.

Alternative 2
Reduce the number of employees by 20%.

HUMAN RESOURCES

Alternative 1
Cancel all training courses.

Alternative 2
Reduce company contributions to the employee pensions and benefits scheme.

FILE 9

UNIT 5 Identifying causes Output task, p47

a Brazilians speak Portuguese, not Spanish.

b Sushi is served raw, not cooked.

c White carnations represent death or bad luck in many parts of Asia. United had to change the colour to red.

d The air in the Middle East was much drier than the air in Taiwan. The hay dried out, became thinner, and gave no protection.

e Eastern block countries boycotted the games that year, so American athletes collected an unusually high number of medals.

f Nova sounds like *no va* which means 'doesn't go' in Spanish – so it wasn't a good name for a car.

FILE 10

UNIT 3 Meetings 4, p29

You work for Hannaford Bros, an American supermarket chain. Your partner works for Yahoo!, the Internet services provider. Ask and answer questions to find out about meetings in each other's companies. Make brief notes in the table.

	Hannaford Bros	Yahoo!
Participants	The top management team, board of directors, and the general counsel (who takes the minutes).	
Frequency	Every two months.	
Purpose	To guide the company to success and profit. (The board gives advice but it doesn't manage.)	
Procedure	Everyone does their homework before the meeting and it's formal. The Chairman runs the meeting and people raise their hands and get permission to speak.	
Location	A hotel in Boston. Directors sit close to the Chairman around a table.	
Dress code	Formal (suits and ties).	
Energy source	Lobster is the favourite.	

FILE 11

UNIT 4 Explanations Output task, p37

File 11

Attention to detail is our speciality. This space shuttle suit is made to exactly the same measurements as a real NASA suit (not just drawings), so it looks like the real thing. We use lightweight plastics and special fabrics to produce high quality replicas that weigh less than 14 kg.

Many of our suits are designed for science museums and for film and television productions, but you could wear this one to explore your neighborhood if you like. It comes with handmade boots for extra-vehicular activity and you don't need to worry about the heat.
Our liquid cooling systems enable you to enjoy the sun. With space suits like these, life is more enjoyable on any planet.

Prices for shuttle suits start at $5,795, and they are also available for rent.

KEY VOCABULARY

fabric material used for making clothes, etc.
a replica an exact copy of something
extra-vehicular activity work outside the space shuttle

FILE 12

UNIT 3 Holding a meeting 2, p35

Tell your partner about these ideas. Discuss whether:

a people are trying similar things in your town or city
b you think it's a good idea or not.

The Italian government is subsidizing the building of underground garages and Trevi Park, an Italian company, has come up with a new approach to parking. They drill very large holes in the ground and install fully-automated parking systems with elevators that can move vertically and horizontally. Nobody needs to park their car themselves any more.

To discourage people from driving, many British cities have park-and-ride schemes. There are free car parks on the edges of cities with subsidized bus services to the city centre. Many cities also have pedestrianized areas in the centre.

The Friday night rush hour in São Paulo is crazy in the summer because lots of people want to leave the city and drive to the beach. To relieve congestion they change the traffic flow systems. Sometimes all eight lanes of the motorways lead out of the city, and travellers trying to get into the city have to use minor roads.

When the Chinese government wanted to reduce traffic near Tiananmen Square by 20% between 7.00 a.m. and 8.00 p.m., they banned hatchback cars. There was no particular reason for choosing hatchbacks, except that 20% of the cars in Beijing happened to be hatchbacks.

KEY VOCABULARY

congestion a situation where roads and streets are crowded and blocked
to discourage to try to stop somebody doing something
a hatchback a car with a door that lifts up at the back
minor roads small or less important roads, not major roads

pedestrianized area a place for people who are walking (pedestrians), and where no cars are allowed
rush hour a period of time in a day when there is a lot of traffic
to subsidize to pay money towards the cost of something

FILE 13

UNIT 5 Anticipating problems 5, p45

Read this extract from the article about the Nintendo helpdesk. Prepare to explain the information to your partner.

The young employees have a high success rate in solving the customers' problems. 'Usually it's got something to do with a remote control button,' explains sixteen-year-old Aaron Barton, as if it's all very easy. 'Or sometimes they've got the line-in, line-out plugs mixed up.'

The teenage staff mostly help customers deal with equipment set-up problems, leaving the regular staff free to deal with questions about the games themselves.

As well as technical support manuals, Nintendo provides the young workers with a list of suggested 'empathy statements'. These include phrases like 'I can relate to how you're feeling', 'I can see that you're upset', and 'I would be feeling frustrated too'. The teenagers read them from the list whenever they need them.

KEY VOCABULARY

empathy the ability to imagine how another person is feeling
frustrated angry or dissatisfied because you can't do what you want
a manual a book that

explains how to operate something
a plug an object which connects wires to electrical equipment
upset unhappy and worried

FILE 14

UNIT 4 Doing research Output task, p43

You are preparing a purchase request for some glass equipment for your research laboratory. Phone Salem Glass and check they have the following items in stock. You only have last year's catalogue so you also need to check if the prices and discounts have changed. Make any necessary changes to your purchase request form. Be careful. There are some problems to solve.

Purchase Request

Date: 27 March

Supplier: Salem Glass Company

Quantity	Description	Ref.no.	Item price	Total price
12	20 mm diameter immersion tubes	I/20	$17.08	$204.96
24	60 mm diameter immersion tubes	I/60	$35.72	$857.28
5	130 ml sulfur absorption tubes	SA/110	$20.06	$100.30
10	Hirsh funnels	G/147	$23.00	$230.00
12	Gooch crucibles	?	$21.70	$260.40
			Less 15% discount	

FILE 15

UNIT 3 Holding a meeting 2, p35

Tell your partner about these ideas. Discuss whether:

a people are trying similar things in your town or city
b you think it's a good idea or not.

The Swiss watch maker, Schweizerische Gesellschaft, and the German luxury car maker, Daimler-Benz, worked together to develop a 'smart car'. It's only 2.5 metres long so it can fit into tiny parking spaces, and it has a base price of $8,500. It covers 100 km on less than five litres of gasoline. Some European cities are dedicating streets to smart car parking.

Athens has an unusual system for reducing weekday traffic. On even-numbered days (for example, the second or fourth of the month) you can only drive cars that have an even number on their licence plate. On odd-numbered days, you can only drive cars with odd-numbered plates.

In Amsterdam, they are experimenting with bicycles that people can pick up in one location and drop off in another. Users have to register first and they then receive a smart card, which slots into the bicycle and keeps track of where they travel.

In many places in the US, only drivers of HOVs can use fast lanes on highways. HOVs are High Occupancy Vehicles, where there are two or more passengers. The goal is to encourage car-pooling.

KEY VOCABULARY

car-pooling a situation where two or more people share one car

to dedicate streets to smart car parking to allow only smart cars to park in particular streets

to drop off to leave something somewhere

an even number a number that can be divided by two, e.g. 2, 4, 6, 8, etc.

gasoline liquid fuel (American English) the British English is *petrol*

a licence plate a car number plate

an odd number a number that can't be divided by two, e.g. 1, 3, 5, 7, etc.

to pick up to collect

a smart card a plastic card that looks similar to a credit card, but contains a microchip that records and remembers information

FILE 16

UNIT 2 Journeys 1, p18

The word *travel* can be a verb.

I travelled by train.

It can also be a noun.

Air travel is making the world a smaller place.

We only use the verb *travel* to talk about the general activity of visiting different places. To talk about going to a particular place, we use the noun *journey*, not travel.

My journey to Tibet was long and difficult.

~~*My travel to Tibet was long and difficult.*~~

We often use the noun *trip* to talk about a whole visit – both the journey and the stay in a particular place.

I'm going on a trip to Paris to meet a customer.

FILE 18

UNIT 5 Anticipating problems 5, p45

Read this extract from the article about the Nintendo helpdesk. Prepare to explain the information to your partner.

> Katie Shaughnessy's last Christmas job was putting groceries in bags at a supermarket for $6 an hour. This year she'll get $9 an hour and a Nintendo game set that retails at $129.99 if she works the full week between Christmas and New Year.
>
> The only other job Aaron Barton's ever had was delivering newspapers, and he can't believe he's getting paid to do this. 'We get a free lunch, plus they have free computer games whenever we go on a break,' he says.
>
> But it seems that other things are important to the kids as well. 'Here I feel I'm getting treated like an adult,' says Aaron. 'It's totally different from high school.' And Katie enjoys the work too. She says, 'It's fun when you can help people.'

KEY VOCABULARY

retail at   to sell for the price of

FILE 17

UNIT 4 Explanations Output task, p37

KEY VOCABULARY

ideal perfect
to recharge to put a new supply of electricity into a battery

File 17

The Street-Wiz Scooter

Now you can save the planet and have fun at the same time. Powered by clean electricity, your Street-Wiz scooter can go as fast as 25 km per hour — ideal for a trip to the shops, avoiding the rush-hour traffic, or just having fun.

The Street-Wiz is very quiet, so your neighbours will love it too. It runs on batteries that are stored over the back wheel. Plug it into the wall for less than six hours and the batteries fully recharge.

When folded up, your Street-Wiz is only 91 cm long and 31 cm high — ideal for fitting into a car, a train, or even on board a plane. It weighs just 18kg with batteries or 9 kg without, so you can take it everywhere.

At a price of only $700, you're going to wonder what you did before you got Street-Wiz!

Tapescript

Unit 1
Organizations

1.1

1 Hello. I'm Alessandro Ponti and I'm a research technician at a hospital here in Torino. I have colleagues from several different countries and we have English lessons twice a week so we can communicate better. I'm married, I have three children, and I like painting and drawing in my free time.

2 Good morning. I'm Michiko Sudo and I work in my family's trading company. Our head office is in Osaka and we have 140 employees. I'm responsible for worldwide sales and marketing, so I need English to talk to our customers.

3 Hello, nice to meet you. I'm Peter Leutwiler and I'm a freelance computer consultant. I specialize in database management for banking and financial services. I live in Frankfurt, and I often travel abroad to attend conferences, or just for fun.

4 Hello, I'm Jean-Philippe Gérard and I work for Eco Industries SA in Compiègne, France. I'm lead operator in the water treatment plant. I also study engineering at the Université de Technologie, and most of the books I need to read are in English.

5 Hi. I'm Sushma Advani and I come from Mumbai in India, but now I work for a recruitment agency in Pittsburgh in the US. Our main client is the US Government, and it employs us to recruit computer programmers from all over the world. In my job, I speak Hindi, Sindi, Marathi, French ... and English, of course.

1.2

1 We provide telephone services to twenty-five million customers, and we're going to move into cable television. We're laying cables across the country and we're going to offer our customers telephone, data, and TV services.

2 We do genetic research – so we study how genes work and why they sometimes go wrong. It's a great challenge. We're trying to identify the genes that cause high blood pressure and heart disease – and some day, we're going to find a cure.

3 We're developing some new software for financial planning. It's difficult to find enough qualified programmers here in the US. So we're setting up a project team in India and we're going to do a lot of the work over there.

4 We're installing robots to reduce our labour costs. But we're also working on our just-in-time system, looking for ways to reduce our inventory. One day we're going to close down this warehouse and save a lot of money.

5 We're storing them here until we can sort them out. It's a big job. We're going to break them down, separate the components, and recycle them. But a lot of the parts are no use and they're going to be scrapped.

1.3

OK, good morning, everybody, and welcome to Brussels. This is the European headquarters of JRB and we now have offices in sixteen cities around the world. Our globalization programme is currently extending into Central Europe and Russia and that's why we're here today. We need reliable communication links with Central Europe, links that guarantee we can communicate with our offices, partners, and clients twenty-four hours a day, every day of the year. And with your help, we're going to create the infrastructure we need.

Now, we have a lot of new faces around the table today so I'd like to begin with some introductions. I'd like everybody to tell us a bit about their company, their position, and their role in this project. Let me start. I'm Helen Chapelle. I'm Vice-President of JRB, responsible for communications, and I'm the director of this project. So I'm going to be in charge of the overall planning and installation of the new communication systems. OK. Alexandro, you're next.

1.4

1 I'm currently based in Jakarta where we're introducing ISO 9000 in our new Indonesian operation. But I'm going to move to Brussels next month to work on this project. I'm going to be working with everyone here to develop reliable operational procedures.

2 We're responsible for providing fast and reliable connections to

the web and for customer support. And we're also responsible for data security. So we're going to develop systems to protect the data and to manage the on-line payments.

3 I've worked for JRB in Europe, the Middle East, and Japan, and my role in this project is to keep things moving. I'm going to prepare schedules, co-ordinate between the local teams and the head office, and make sure we do everything on time and within budget.

4 Our head office is in St. Paul, Minnesota, and we provide domestic and international satellite services. We offer voice, fax, and data transmission and we also provide system design, installation, and technical support services.

5 We're based in Budapest and we have a lot of experience in Eastern Europe. We help companies introduce change, and deal with problems in the new business climate of this region. Our main strength is our local knowledge and we have many contacts with government agencies in Russia.

Unit 2
Visitors

2.1

A Is there a lot of crime in Beijing?
B No, China's a very safe country to visit. Is it your first trip?
A Yes. Tell me, what kind of clothing should I take?
B When are you going?
A Next week.
B OK. It's very hot there at the moment. You'll need summer clothes.
A What about business meetings?

What do people wear?
B They're practical rather than formal. You should take a suit to be on the safe side, but you don't need to wear a jacket all the time. A short-sleeved shirt is fine.
A Oh, good. Do many people speak English?
B No, very few. Do you have an interpreter?
A Yes.
B Good, you'll need one.
A Is it difficult doing business in Beijing?
B It takes time. You have to get to know your contacts.
A Yes, I hear you need to be patient.
B That's right. You shouldn't try to rush things.
A OK. What happens at business meetings?
B Well, people usually arrive early and they start by exchanging business cards.
A Yes, I got some printed with Chinese writing on the back.
B Good. You need to exchange cards with both hands and study them carefully.
A And do the meetings start on time?
B Well, you shouldn't discuss business too soon. There's usually some polite conversation over tea to start with.
A Mm, I see. What happens next?

2.2

A Hi, Louise, it's Jean-François. Have you got a moment?
B Yes, of course. Is it about next week's visit?
A Yes. I've organized your programme but there are a few things I'd like to check.
B Sure.
A Great. Now, you're arriving here on Tuesday at nine o'clock.
B Ah, I'm afraid I'm going to be a little late, perhaps about ten?
A OK, ten o'clock then. That's no problem. Nathalie Rousseau, our Chief Operating Officer, would

like to meet you when you arrive, then you have meetings with the marketing team.
B Excellent.
A Do you want to see round the Grenoble facility in the afternoon?
B Yes, please. I'd like that.
A Good. Then, if you're not too tired, Antoine Boirin, our Purchasing Manager, would like to have dinner with you in the evening. There's a nice seafood restaurant at the port ...
B Oh, I'm afraid I'm allergic to seafood.
A OK, no problem. We could make it ... let's see ... would you like to go to a Thai restaurant instead?
B Mm, that sounds nice.
A Fine, I'll change the booking.
B Great.
A Then on Wednesday morning, you're visiting one of our clients. That's Morin Pharmaceutique.
B Oh, I'm sorry, but I went to Morin last time I came. There's another company, though ... I think it's Armagen?
A Armagen?
B Yes, that's it.
A So do you want me to cancel Morin Pharmaceutique and arrange a visit to Armagen instead?
B Yes, could you do that?
A Fine. It should be no problem.
B Thanks a lot.
A Then the afternoon is free but perhaps you'd like to see something of the city?
B That'd be very nice. I didn't have time on my last visit.
A Then I'll arrange a tour.
B That's very kind of you.
A Now, you're not doing anything in the evening. Would you like me to arrange anything for you?
B I'd prefer to leave it free, if that's OK.
A No problem.
B Is that everything, then?
A Yes, I think so.

B Well, thank you very much for arranging all this, Jean-François.

A Oh, you're very welcome. Thank you for coming.

2.3

A It all starts with a basic idea – a few sketches on the back of an envelope.

B Really?

A Sure, well, kind of. We work the sketches up into a full-size drawing and then we move it over on to these computers.

B Do you use CAD-CAM programs?

A Yes. We have some very sophisticated computers here to create the images – these cost nearly a million bucks a piece. They create 3-D models and what's really great is they can make all kinds of early calculations, like how the car will perform in a crash.

B I see. And what happens next?

A The next step is to make a clay model of the car. Come over here and I'll show you one ...

B Why do you use clay?

A It's easy to build up and take off, so we can experiment.

B And you try to improve the aerodynamics?

A Yes. Aerodynamics is the key thing. It has to cut through the air.

B So these clay models aren't life size?

A No, they're about one-fifth of the real size, but that's big enough to test in a wind tunnel.

B OK.

A Then, after that, we build a fibreglass model and that's full size.

B I see. And do you show it to prospective buyers?

A Yeah. We use the fibreglass model for market research, and we use it for more tests, too. We put it in a wind tunnel again. Come with me and I'll show you ... It's too late to make major changes to the design by this stage. But we can improve things like mirrors, wheels, bumpers ...

B To improve the aerodynamics?

A That's right. We also work on the suspension system, fine-tuning it to make sure the car will be comfortable and hold the road well. Then after that, we produce a real car and test that.

B Do you have a test track here?

A No, we have one in Death Valley in California. We can test the car over different road conditions there.

B Before it goes into production?

A Yes, production's the final stage.

B And tell me, do you use a lot of robots on the assembly line?

A Yeah, these days the cars are all built by robots. There are very few people on the assembly line and they're usually checking quality.

Unit 3
Sharing ideas

3.1

A Here it is. What do you think?

B Very nice.

C Yes, I like it.

D Hm, I'm not sure about the colour.

B Could we make it in different colours ... yellow, green, blue?

A Sure.

B Then the kids can collect the set.

A That's a great idea.

B What colours are best?

D We could do some market research to find out.

C It'll take too long. And we already know kids like bright colours best, so I don't think it's worth it.

A Why don't we just choose three or four bright colours, then?

B Fine.

C Yes.

A OK. What about the face?

B I like the mouth.

D But it doesn't look very friendly.

C How about making the eyes bigger?

B That'll work.

A OK. So we want bigger eyes. Do you agree, Sara?

D Yes, bigger eyes, but I think it's a toy for boys. Couldn't we make a different toy for girls?

C But we've talked about this before. The market research results are quite clear.

A Yes, we know the kids want an alien.

D But how can the girls play with it? It doesn't do anything.

B What about putting a noise-maker in the bottom, so it makes a sound if you squeeze it?

D Good idea.

A That means having two pieces.

C It's too complicated. We can't afford it.

D Are you sure?

A I think we should look into it.

B I agree. It's worth investigating.

A OK. I'll get some price estimates.

D And I think we should give it something extra – perhaps a hat to put on and take off.

C Aliens don't wear hats.

D How do you know? Have you ever met one?

A OK, let's check it out. I'll go back to the designers and see what they can do.

3.2

A I think you should base the price on costs.

B Yes, but it also depends on our market strategy.

A Yes, but the margin's the key thing. If you take your material costs and add 60%, that covers the operating costs and gives you a 20% profit. It's a good formula.

B Yes, but what about our competitors? How much are they charging?

3.3

A We must make sure our price is lower than anyone else's.

B Mm, I'm not sure if that's necessary.

A We can't sell it if the price is too high.

B I don't think that's true. Our model's better than any of our competitors'.

A But if we charge less, we sell more.

B Perhaps.

A So we have more money coming in.

B But we might not make as much profit.

3.4

A I think we should charge at least 10% more than the competition.

B Why's that?

A We built a lot of energy-saving features into the design. So it costs less to operate than our competitors' products.

B Yes, the running costs are lower.

A Yeah, it's 10% more efficient than anything else on the market.

B Mm. It'll reduce our customers' energy bills.

A Exactly. They'll spend a lot less on electricity.

B And in the long run, they'll save money.

A That's right.

Unit 4
Exchanging
information

4.1

A Is this a jet-ski?

B No, it's the opposite of a jet-ski – it travels under the water instead of on top.

A What's it for?

B You can use it to explore shipwrecks, study fish, whatever you want, really.

A So it's similar to a submarine.

B Yes, it's like a one-person submarine. It enables you to dive down under the sea.

A How far?

B Up to thirteen metres.

A It looks like a space suit. How long can you stay under water?

B It's designed for dives of about fifty minutes. There's an air supply inside so you can breathe normally.

A How fast can it go?

B About four kilometres per hour. It has a small electric motor.

A Uh-huh.

B And it runs on a rechargeable 12-volt battery.

A What's it made of?

B I'm not sure. Some kind of plastic, I think.

A And how much does it cost?

B Only twenty-two thousand dollars.

A Hmm …

4.2

Can you say the alphabet, like this?
A B C D E F G H I J K L M N O P Q R S T U V W X Y, and finally, in British English, we say Zed.

And in American English, we say Zee.

4.3

a A Sorry, I didn't catch your number.

B It's nine seven six eight oh four.

A Did you say eight oh four?

B Yes, that's right.

b A Is that everything?

B Yes, I think so.

A Could we run through it again?

B Sure.

A OK, so it's twenty pieces, reference number H three nine six.

B Yes.

A And thirty pieces, reference number G six four two.

B Er, no, J six four two.

c A Wow! What a good price!

B Sorry?

A Thirteen dollars!

B No, it costs thirty dollars.

A So it's not a good price, then?

B No, it's not.

d A How about three-thirty?

B Yes, three-thirty is fine with me.

A Good. See you on the sixth at three-thirty, then.

B The sixth? I thought we said the sixteenth.

A Oh, yes, you're right.

e A Could you say that again?

B Yes, I don't have all the fax.

A So you mean you need more information?

B No, I mean the last two pages of the fax didn't arrive.

4.4

A This is the mail box of …

B Carmen Muñoz.

A Please leave your message after the tone.

C Hi, Carmen, this is Seth. I'm just calling to bring you up to date on the corporate safety video. I've prepared a budget and I've included costs for translation into five languages. I've also included travel to Africa and Japan. I'm planning to shoot the film at our plants there. I just need you to authorize the budget for me. Let me know when you've signed it. Thanks. Catch you later.

4.5

Seth, this is Carmen calling about the corporate safety video. This budget's much too big! We can't afford to pay for travel to Africa or Japan. You'll have to shoot the film in the States. Use our plant in Denver or Philadelphia. Give me a call if you want to talk about this.

4.6

Carmen, it's Seth again. We keep missing one another. Listen, this video is going to be used all over the world. It has to make sense to machine operators in places like Nairobi and Osaka. They aren't going to learn much about safety if they're looking at machines in a plant in Denver. Please give me a call when you get a chance.

4.7

Seth? Carmen. I've just spoken to our plant in Philadelphia and they have the machines you need. Could you get in touch with Chuck Swier and set a date? He's the plant manager in Philadelphia and he knows all about the machines and safety procedures. Chuck's number is 215 555 7693. Let me know what date you decide on.

4.8

Seth, this is Carmen again. How are things going with the corporate safety video? Have you gotten in touch with Chuck Swier yet? Bring me up to date as soon as you can.

4.9

Hi, Carmen, it's Seth, calling to update you on the corporate training video. Sorry I didn't call you yesterday but I was tied up on the project. I've spoken to Chuck in Philadelphia and we've set a date. We're going to shoot the film on the fourteenth. I've hired a camera operator and booked our flights. I haven't rented the equipment yet, but I'll do that when we get there. There's something else, though. Chuck says that all the machine operators in Philadelphia are Caucasian men. We can't have all white guys on the video. It's just not right, so I've hired some actors – African-Americans and Asians. Now this is going to cost extra, but not as much as travelling to Africa and Asia. So

I've done a new budget and I need you to sign it. I'll email it to you now and maybe you could fax it back to me. Thanks. Catch you later.

4.10

A Hello, Platinum Systems.
B Vic Santoro, please.
A Who's calling, please?
B Chris Frantz from Marketing in Austria.
C Vic Santoro.
B Hi, Vic, it's Chris.
C Oh, hello, Chris. What can I do for you?
B We've got a problem.
C What's up?
B It's the leaflets for the exhibition. They're not here.
C You mean they haven't arrived in Vienna yet?
B No, and the exhibition opens on Monday.
C That's strange. They were sent last Wednesday.
B Then why aren't they here?
C Have you contacted the freight company?
B No, I thought it was your responsibility.
C OK. I'll call them and find out what's happened.
B Thanks. Could you do it right away?
C Sure, I'll call you back as soon as I have any information.
B Do you know my extension number?
C Yes, I have it here. Was there anything else?
B No, that's all. I'll wait to hear from you, then.
C Yes, sure.
B Thanks a lot. Bye.

4.11

A Then why aren't they here?
A Then why aren't they here?

B Then where are they?
B Then where are they?

C Well, we don't have them.
C Well, we don't have them.

D Well, they never made it here.
D Well, they never made it here.

Unit 5
Solving problems

5.1

A What's happening in Japan?
B Sales are still down.
A I wonder why.
B Well, the price can't be the problem. It's very competitive.
A Maybe we've priced it too low.
B Why do you say that?
A Well, it might be that people equate price with quality.
B No, Japanese consumers are looking for value these days.
A OK, so why didn't the promotion work?
B It must have been the advertisement.
A Yes, but what's wrong with it?
B That's the problem. We're not sure.
A What about the wording? Was the translation OK?
B Yes, we checked.
A Perhaps it was because of that line about the four-litre bottles.
B What's wrong with that?
A Four is an unlucky number in Japan, isn't it?
B Yes, it is. Maybe that was the problem, then.
A Or perhaps four-litre bottles are just too big. Japanese homes don't have much storage space.
B Then the size is wrong?
A Yes, possibly.
B Hey, there's something else.
A What's that?
B Well, I'm not sure, but it could have been because people read the pictures from bottom to top, instead of top to bottom.
A That's confusing.
B What do you think? Can we check it out?

5.2

A So are we going to buy this software?

B We haven't decided yet.

A Is the cost the problem?

B No. If it works, we'll recoup our initial investment in three years.

A Then what's stopping us?

B It's a big decision. This software will integrate all our activities – purchasing, manufacturing, logistics, customer order management ... everything.

A But that's a good thing, right?

B Yes, we'll have much more information about the market.

A So what's the problem?

B Well, if we go ahead and buy it, we'll have to re-engineer the whole company. It means changing all our systems so they work with the software.

A Why can't the software work with our current systems?

B It's not designed that way.

A So we have to adapt to the software?

B That's right.

A It'll be difficult to implement all the changes.

B Very difficult. It'll take at least a year.

A I see. So what happens if we don't buy this software?

B Well, nothing. We'll go on working like we do now.

A We won't have to change anything.

B And we'll be able to go home on time at night.

A Well, the software we have now works OK.

B Yes, at the moment.

A And what are our competitors doing?

B They're buying this software.

A So, if we don't buy it, we might lose our competitive edge.

B Yes. The thing is, it's a very powerful business tool, but it's risky. If the implementation process goes smoothly, it'll be fantastic. But if it takes too long, it could put us out of business.

5.3

A We need to fill out some time sheets.

C But we've already filled out time sheets.

D Yes, but they were for the bookkeepers.

A That's right, Isabelle. They weren't detailed enough for the project manager.

B What else does he want to know?

A How far we've gotten with the project.

C Well, we're about halfway through.

A No, he needs figures for every task.

B Every task in the project?

A Yes.

B That'll take at least two days.

D Who is going to be responsible for this?

A How about you, Christophe?

B I'm behind schedule already. I'm afraid I can't take on any more work at the moment.

A Isabelle?

D I'm tied up too. I've got meetings every day this week. Sorry.

A Can you do it, Paul?

C What exactly do you want me to do?

A We need percentage figures for how much work is completed.

C For each task in the project?

A Yes. How long will it take you?

D I'll send you my files. They're all up to date.

B Yes, I can send you mine as well.

A OK, that's good. And the project manager wants an update. You're good at progress reports Paul, so maybe you could do that too?

C A progress report as well?

A Yes. How soon can you do it?

C But I'm going on a training course for the rest of this week.

A How's your schedule in the evenings? Can you do it by Friday?

C You want time sheets and a progress report by Friday?

A That's the deadline.

C OK.

A That's great. Thanks, Paul.

5.4

A This is a confidential message to ...

B Jackie Halliday.

A from ...

C Rod Lapinski,

A Chief Executive Officer.

C Jackie. I can't make tomorrow's meeting, so I'd like you to chair it. I've drafted some proposals for discussion. Please look through them tonight and see if you can come up with some more ideas. OK ... Now, this is how I want you to run the meeting. First we need to review our strategy. What are our long-term and short-term plans? If we make bigger cuts in some departments, we can invest the money in others. So start the meeting with a discussion of strategy. After that, move on to the budget cuts. Go through my draft proposals one by one. I want to know what ideas other people have as well, so find out what everybody at the meeting thinks. Try to get agreement on this, Jackie. I want everybody committed to the plan. Now, we can't make any final decisions until we have accurate figures. The department heads need to work these out as soon as possible. So before you finish the meeting, make sure everyone knows what they need to do next, and by when. We can't afford delays on this. OK. I think that's it. I'll call you tomorrow and find out how it went.

Glossary

accurate correct and exact

an acquaintance a person you know who is not a close friend

across the board affecting all departments, involving everyone

an advantage a good point, a strength

an advertisement publicity designed to sell a product or service

to afford to have enough money to pay for something

an alternative a choice, an option

to award to give a prize. Also a noun: *an award*

based located, situated in a particular placed

a battery a device which stores and provides electricity

a benefit something good that a company gives its employees, for example, health insurance or a company car

a booking a reservation

bookkeeping keeping records of the money that a business spends and receives

to brainstorm to solve problems by asking members of a group to think of as many ideas as possible

a budget an amount of money you plan to spend for a special purpose. Also *within budget* – not overspending; and *to budget for something* – to plan to spend an amount of money on something

a calendar a list showing the days, weeks, and months of the year. In British English, a calendar is something you hang on a wall. An appointment book is called a *diary*. In American English, this book is called a *calendar*.

a campaign a plan to do a number of things in order to achieve a goal, for example an advertising campaign

to cancel to say an appointment or a meeting won't happen

cash flow the movement of money in and out of a business

a catalogue a list of all the things you can buy from a company

CEO Chief Executive Officer

to chair a meeting to run or control a meeting

to circulate to pass from one person to another

a client someone who receives a service

a code a group of numbers used for identification: 'First dial 44 – that's the code for the UK.'

a colleague a person who works with you in the same organization or group

to come up with to find or produce an answer

commercial connected with buying and selling goods

to be committed to be convinced that something is right and important and therefore be willing to give it a lot of your time and effort

a competitor another company operating in the same area of the market. Also *competitive prices* and *competitive edge*

a component a part of a product

confidential private, secret

confirmation a statement that something is true or correct

a consumer a person who buys goods or services

to contribute to give money, ideas, etc. to help make something successful. Also a noun: *a contribution*

a cost an expense, money that has to be spent

credit terms arrangements for paying for goods or services at a later time

currency the money system of a country

currency fluctuations changes in the value of a currency

a customer someone who buys a product

to cut to reduce

a cut a reduction

to cut back – to reduce spending, etc.

D (in dimensions) depth, how deep something is

a deadline a time or date before which something must be done

to deliver to take something to a particular place

demand how much customers want goods or services

a department a section of a company, usually organized by function: 'She works in the Human Resources Department.'

a dimension a measurement of size

direct mail advertising material posted to a named person

a discount a price reduction

a division a section of a company, usually organized by geographical area or products

domestic inside your own country

downtime time when equipment is not operational

a draft a first or early version of a document that can be changed

an economist a person who studies economics – the way money, trade, and industry are organized

efficient working well and quickly, producing a good result in the minimum time. Also an adverb: *efficiently*

to employ to give work to someone. Also *employer* (the company), *employee* (the worker), and *employment*

to enable to make something possible

to export to send goods to another country for sale

to extend to make something bigger or longer

an extension a direct telephone line in a building with many telephone lines

a facility a building where work is done. Also plural: *facilities* – rooms, equipment, or services

a fare the amount of money you have to pay for a ticket to travel

fertilizer a chemical substance you put on soil to make things grow

a file a box or cover used for keeping papers together, or a collection of information on paper or a computer

to fire to dismiss a worker from their job

finance the management of money. Also a verb: *to finance* – to provide money to pay for something

financial connected with money

freight carrying goods from one place to another

fund-raising organizing events to get money for something

global worldwide

a guarantee a promise to repair or replace a product that is not satisfactory. Also a verb: *to guarantee*

a gym a gymnasium, a large room with equipment for doing physical exercise

Guinness the company that monitors world record-breaking attempts

H (in dimensions) height, how high something is

headquarters the main office of a company

a helpdesk a section of a company that helps customers with problems over the telephone

to hire to employ new workers, to pay someone to do a job

a hypermarket a very large supermarket

to implement to put a plan into action. Also a noun: *implementation*

to import to bring goods into a country from abroad

to install to put equipment in place so it's ready for use. Also a noun: *installation*

an invoice a list of goods sold with a request for payment

an item a subject or thing. 'The next item on the agenda is ...'

an itinerary a plan for a visit or journey, showing places, dates, times, and people to see

labour costs money paid to workers for their services

to launch to introduce a new product to a market

a leaflet a printed piece of paper that advertises or gives information about something

a leakage a situation where liquid or gas gets through a small hole

legal connected with the law

a lift a ride in a car

to link to form a connection. Also a noun: *a link*

to load to put goods onto a truck, train, plane, etc.

a locomotive a machine that pulls a train

logistics the organization of supplies and services

to look into to investigate (something)

mail post, letters, and parcels

maintenance keeping something in good working order

to manufacture to make things in large quantities using machines

a market a geographical area or a section of the population where you can sell your products

market research the study of what people want to buy and why

market segments sections of the market

a model a copy of something, usually smaller than the real thing. Also one of the products that is sold or made by a company: 'The Daytona has been one of Triumph's most successful models.'

overtime time spent at work after normal working hours

to pack to put goods in boxes ready for transport or sale

a passenger a person who travels on a plane, in cars, etc.

pensions money paid regularly to people who have finished their working lives

a plant a large factory

a porter someone who carries bags in a hotel, airport, etc.

a price the amount of money you must pay to buy something

profit the money made by a business, total sales minus total costs Also *to make a profit* – to make more money than you spend; *profitable* – making a profit

a promotion a special event to advertise something

to protect to keep something safe

to provide to give, to offer

to publish to prepare and print a book, or newspaper

to purchase to buy

quality how good or bad something is

a range a group of products sold by one company

to recruit to employ or take on new employees. Also a noun: *recruitment*

to reduce to make lower or smaller. Also a noun: *a reduction*

relevant connected with what is happening or being talked about

reliable always working well and not likely to fail

to rent to pay to use something for a period of time

to retail to sell to the public in shops, stores, supermarkets, etc.

reputation the opinion that people generally have about what something is like

revenue turnover, money from sales

a role a function someone has, a part someone plays

to run to operate, to organize

a salary money you earn for doing a job, usually paid monthly

a satellite an object sent into space to circle the Earth

a schedule a plan of work that must be done Also *behind schedule* – doing things later than the time you planned; *ahead of schedule* – doing things earlier than you planned

a share a part of something that belongs to you or you are responsible for, for example: 'Our market share increased'. Also *shared* – divided up, *shared costs* – costs that are paid by more than one person

a shareholder a person who owns shares in a company and so can have some of the profits

a shift a division of the working day, for example, an eight-hour shift

a shipment a quantity of goods being transported from one place to another

specifications details and / or instructions describing design and materials

a state-owned company a company that belongs to a state or government – not privately owned

storage space a place where you can keep or store things

a strategy a plan you use in order to achieve something

to supply to provide customers with goods

a task a particular piece of work

theft the crime of stealing

tied up busy

time sheets documents that show how much time workers have spent on particular tasks

in time not late

on time at the correct time

a tip an extra amount of money you give to a waiter, taxi driver, etc. Also a verb: *to tip*

a tool a piece of software or equipment that helps you to do a job

trade buying and selling. Also *a trade union* – a workers' organization

training teaching somebody how to do a job

an update a report on the current state of things. Also a verb: *to update* and *to bring someone up to date*

to upgrade to change to a better, more advanced system

a vehicle something that transports people from place to place

W (in dimensions) – width, how wide something is

a wage money you earn for working in a job – usually paid weekly to manual workers

white goods domestic appliances such as refrigerators, washing machines, dishwashers, etc.

a workload an amount of work you have to do

to be worth having a particular value in money, for example: 'The price is $500, but it's only worth $50.'

yen the currency of Japan

OXFORD
UNIVERSITY PRESS

Great Clarendon Street, Oxford OX2 6DP

Oxford University Press is a department of the University of Oxford. It furthers the University's objective of excellence in research, scholarship, and education by publishing worldwide in

Oxford New York

Athens Auckland Bangkok Bogotá Buenos Aires Calcutta Cape Town Chennai Dar es Salaam Delhi Florence Hong Kong Istanbul Karach Kuala Lumpur Madrid Melbourne Mexico City Mumbai Nairobi Paris São Paulo Singapore Taipei Tokyo Toronto Warsaw

with associated companies in Berlin Ibadan

Oxford and Oxford English are registered trade marks of Oxford University Press in the UK and in certain other countries

© Oxford University Press 2000

The moral rights of the author have been asserted

Database right Oxford University Press (maker)

First published 2000

ISBN 0 19 457292 7

Printed in Hong Kong

Acknowledgements

The authors and publisher are grateful to those who have given permission to reproduce the following extracts and adaptations of copyright material:

pp 18–19 'Triumphant biker returns' appeared in Focus magazine, August 1997 edition, reproduced by permission of Gruner & Jahr (UK) Partners.
p 26 Intuit Inc. website
p 28 Adaptation of 'The meeting I never miss' by Matt Goldberg. Reprinted with permission from Fast Company magazine © by Fast Company. All rights reserved.
pp 45, 59, 61 Adapted extracts taken from 'Plugged-in students help adults stymied by games' by Sam Howe Verhovek. Appeared in the New York Times, 31 December 1998.

Although every effort has been made to trace and contact copyright holders before publication, this has not always been possible. We apologize for any apparent infringement of copyright and if notified the publisher will be pleased to rectify any errors or omissions at the earliest opportunity.

Illustrations by:

Nigel Paige pp 22, 47, 50, 51
Technical Graphics, OUP pp 18 (map), 33 (flags), 43

The publishers would like to thank the following for their kind permission to reproduce photographs:

BOB p 36 (The Breathing Observation Bubble)
The Body Shop p 6 (The Body Shop International PLC 1998)
Burnette, Jonathan p 10 (laying cables)
Davis Larry/New York Times Pictures p 45 (helping with video games)
Ecoscene p 35 (London traffic/Amanda Gazidis)
Electrolux p 6 (fridge)
Fed Ex p 6 (Fed Ex)
Finis Inc. pp 37 (Monofin), 56 (Monofin in action)
Hawkins Bazaar pp 30–31
Intuit p 26 (Future is me image)
Katz Pictures p 4 ('Alessandro Ponti'/Donatello Brogioni/Contrasto)
The Kobal Collection p 49 (The Avengers/David Appleby)
Mattel p 28 (BARBIE and associated trademarks are owned by Mattel, Inc. © 1998 Mattel, Inc. All Rights Reserved. Photos Courtesy of Mattel.)

News International plc p 6 (newspapers)
Nintendo UK plc p 44 (games on a tray)
Novartis Consumer Health p 6 (Nicotinell packets)
Photodisc p 8 (baton), p 52 (appointment sheets), cover (meetings, taxi)
Popperfoto p 49 (painting signs on window)
Rex Features pp 6 (Crédit Lyonnais, oil rig, VW Beetle), 35 (cyclists), 37 (scooter/Clive Dixon), 61 (scooter)
Southwest Airlines pp 12–13
SpaceProps pp 37, 58
Still Pictures pp 16 (cyclists/Hartmut Schwarzbach), 35 (traffic/Hartmut Schwarzbach)
The Stock Market p 49 (head in file drawer/James Marvy)
Superstock Ltd pp 8 (cogs), 49 (man in deckchair)
Taiwan Power Company p 6 (power station)
Telegraph Colour Library pp 4 ('Peter Leutwiler'/Nick Clements, 'Jean-Phillipe Gérard'/Antonio Mo, 'Sushma Advani'/V.C.L.), 8 (dartboard/David Burch), 14 and cover (businessman/V.C.L.)
Tony Stone Images pp 4 (female executive/Walter Hodges), 6 (telephone operator), 8 (crowd/Reza Estakhrian, graph/Stephen Johnson), 10 (warehouse/Bruce Foster, businessmen/Jeff Zaruba, computer keyboards/Peter Poulides, technician/Mark Joseph), 27 (David Joel), 29 (informal meeting/Bruce Ayres), 42 (flasks and beakers/Andy Whale), 49 (ladybirds/Tom Bean), cover (businessmen walking/Leland Bobbe, factory workers/Bruce Ayres)
Vauxhall Motors Limited p 24
Wyndham-Leigh Limited p 18

Commissioned photography by:

Haddon Davies pp 32, 46

Designed by Shireen Nathoo Design, London

The author and publisher would also like to thank the following individuals and institutions for their help and advice in the preparation of this book:

The staff and students at EF Corporate Executive Language Schools in Cambridge, UK and Boston, USA; Marcella Banchetti; Maria Barbas Gonzalez; Monica Baumgartner; Carolina Bell; Caroline Boyd Reyes; John Bradley; Brian Brennan; Stephen Brewer; Anna Cole; Tracy Coles; Coprom Langues, Paris; Brian Cross; Europa Formation, Paris; Nadia Fairbrother; Hazel Flack; John Green; Nicola Haughton; Simon Hobson; Sian Howells; International House, Milan; Roger Huntington; Judith Irigoin; Simon Kelway; Michael Kennedy; Martine Lacaze; Sally Lack; Adrian Lefaure; Annie Lyons; Angela Martinez; David Massey; Vicki Moore; Kate Murphy; Raquel de Nicolas; Brian Nield; Steven Pragnell; Bob Ratto; Cesar Sauz; The Sound House, London; SPLEF, Paris; Sharon Statt; Ian Stride; Margaret Swann; Audrey Tirado; Niamh Browne Tixier; Mark Turner; Richard Turner; Anne Vernon-James; Alexander Villiers & Associates; Tania Webster; York Consultants, Paris.